Logical
Operations℠

select

Book

Assessment

eBook

Microsoft® Office
Word 2010

Level 1

Microsoft® Office
Word 2010

Level 1

Microsoft® Office Word 2010: Level 1

Part Number: 084582
Course Edition: 1.0

NOTICES

What is the Microsoft Office Specialist Certification Program?

The Microsoft Office Specialist (MOS) Certification Program enables candidates to show that they have something exceptional to offer - proven expertise in Microsoft® Office programs. The MOS Certification Program is the only Microsoft-approved certification program of its kind. The MOS Certification exams focus on validating specific skill sets within each of the Microsoft® Office system programs. The candidate can choose which exam(s) they want to take according to which skills they want to validate. The available MOS exams include:

- MOS: Microsoft® Office Word 2010
- MOS: Microsoft® Office Excel 2010
- MOS: Microsoft® Office PowerPoint 2010
- MOS: Microsoft® Office Outlook 2010
- MOS: Microsoft® Office Access 2010
- MOS: Microsoft® SharePoint 2010

For more information:

To learn more about MOS or MOS Expert exams, visit **www.microsoft.com/learning/en/us/certification/mos.aspx**.

HELP US IMPROVE OUR COURSEWARE

Your comments are important to us. Please contact us at Element K Press LLC, 1-800-478-7788, 500 Canal View Boulevard, Rochester, NY 14623, Attention: Product Planning, or through our Web site at **http://support.elementkcourseware.com**.

To learn about other MOS or MOS Expert approved courseware from Element K, visit **www.elementkcourseware.com**

* The availability of Microsoft Certified exams varies by Microsoft Office program, program version and language. Visit **www.microsoft.com/learning/en/us/default.aspx** for exam availability.

Microsoft, the Office Logo, Outlook, and PowerPoint are either registered trademarks or trademarks of Microsoft Corporation in the United States and/or other countries. The MOS and MOS Expert Logos are used under license from Microsoft Corporation.

Microsoft® Office Word 2010: Level 1

Lesson 5: Organizing Data in Tables

Lesson 6: Proofing a Word Document

Lesson 7: Controlling the Appearance of Pages in a Word Document

Lesson 8: Printing Word Documents

Appendix A: Microsoft Office Word 2010

Appendix B: Microsoft Office Word Expert 2010

About This Course

Most of the organization maintain and manage large amount of documents. The contents in the document can be stored, enhanced and managed using the Word application and its associated tools. In this course, you will examine the basic concepts of creating a document, editing a document and enhancing a document and its contents by using the Microsoft® Office Word 2010 application.

In the present job scenario, preparing documents for official purpose has become a day-to-day routine. It is also necessary to present the document in a structured manner without any grammatical and other typographical errors, so that the readers find it easy to read through the content. Using Word 2010 for preparing documents can give a better look and feel to your documents.

Course Description

Target Student

This course is designed for students who wish to learn the basic operations of the Microsoft Word to perform their day-to-day responsibilities, and who want to use the application to be more productive in their work. It provides the fundamental knowledge and techniques needed to advance to using more complex Word features such as protecting your documents and usage of ligatures.

Course Prerequisites

To be successful in this course, you should be familiar with using personal computers and you should have used the mouse and keyboard. You should be comfortable in the Windows environment and be able to use Windows to manage information on the computer. Specifically, you should be able to launch and close programs; navigate to information stored on the computer; and manage files and folders. To ensure your success, we recommend you first take one of Element K's introductory Windows courses, such as either of the following, or have equivalent skills and knowledge.

- *Windows XP Professional: Level 1*
- *Windows XP: Introduction*

Course Objectives

In this course, you will create, edit, and enhance standard business documents using Microsoft® Office Word 2010.

You will:

- Identify and work with basic Word 2010 tools and features.
- Edit text in a Word document.
- Modify the appearance of text in a Word document.
- Insert special characters and graphical objects.
- Organize data in tables.
- Proof a Word document.
- Control the appearance of pages in a Word document.
- Print a Word document.

Certification

This course is designed to help you prepare for the following certification.

Certification Path: MOS: Microsoft Office Word 2010 Exam 77–881

Certification Path: MOS: Microsoft Office Word Expert 2010 Exam 77–887

This course is one of a series of Element K courseware titles that addresses Microsoft Office Specialist (MOS) certification skill sets. The MOS and certification program is for individuals who use Microsoft's business desktop software and who seek recognition for their expertise with specific Microsoft products.

How to Use This Book

As a Learning Guide

This book is divided into lessons and topics, covering a subject or a set of related subjects. In most cases, lessons are arranged in order of increasing proficiency.

The results-oriented topics include relevant and supporting information you need to master the content. Each topic has various types of activities designed to enable you to practice the guide-lines and procedures as well as to solidify your understanding of the informational material presented in the course.

At the back of the book, you will find a glossary of the definitions of the terms and concepts used throughout the course. You will also find an index to assist in locating information within the instructional components of the book.

In the Classrom

This book is intended to enhance and support the in-class experience. Procedures and guide-lines are presented in a concise fashion along with activities and discussions. Information is provided for reference and reflection in such a way as to facilitate understanding and practice.

Each lesson may also include a Lesson Lab or various types of simulated activities. You will find the files for the simulated activities along with the other course files on the enclosed CD-ROM. If your course manual did not come with a CD-ROM, please go to **http:// elementkcourseware.com** to download the files. If included, these interactive activities enable you to practice your skills in an immersive business environment, or to use hardware and software resources not available in the classroom. The course files that are available on the CD-ROM or by download may also contain sample files, support files, and additional reference materials for use both during and after the course.

As a Teaching Guide

Effective presentation of the information and skills contained in this book requires adequate preparation. As such, as an instructor, you should familiarize yourself with the content of the entire course, including its organization and approaches. You should review each of the student activities and exercises so you can facilitate them in the classroom.

Throughout the book, you may see Instructor Notes that provide suggestions, answers to problems, and supplemental information for you, the instructor. You may also see references to "Additional Instructor Notes" that contain expanded instructional information; these notes appear in a separate section at the back of the book. PowerPoint slides may be provided on the included course files, which are available on the enclosed CD-ROM or by download from **http://elementkcourseware.com.** The slides are also referred to in the text. If you plan to use the slides, it is recommended to display them during the corresponding content as indicated in the Instructor Notes in the margin.

The course files may also include assessments for the course, which can be administered diagnostically before the class, or as a review after the course is completed. These exam-type questions can be used to gauge the students' understanding and assimilation of course content.

As a Review Tool

Any method of instruction is only as effective as the time and effort you, the student, are willing to invest in it. In addition, some of the information that you learn in class may not be important to you immediately, but it may become important later. For this reason, we encourage you to spend some time reviewing the content of the course after your time in the classroom.

As a Reference

The organization and layout of the book make it easy to use as a learning tool and as an after-class reference. You can use this book as a first source for definitions of terms, background information on given topics, and summaries of procedures.

If your book did not come with a CD, please go to **http:// www.elementk.com/ courseware-file-downloads** to download the data files.

Course Icons

Icon	Description
	A **Caution Note** makes students aware of potential negative consequences of an action, setting, or decision that are not easily known.
	Display Slide provides a prompt to the instructor to display a specific slide. Display Slides are included in the Instructor Guide only.
	An **Instructor Note** is a comment to the instructor regarding delivery, classroom strategy, classroom tools, exceptions, and other special considerations. Instructor Notes are included in the Instructor Guide only.
	Notes Page indicates a page that has been left intentionally blank for students to write on.
	A **Student Note** provides additional information, guidance, or hints about a topic or task.
	A **Version Note** indicates information necessary for a specific version of software.

Course Requirements

Hardware

For this course, you will need one computer for each student and the instructor. Each computer should have the following hardware configuration:

- A 1 GHz Pentium-class processor or faster.
- A minimum of 256 MB of RAM. (512 MB of RAM is recommended.)
- A 10 GB hard disk or larger. You should have at least 1 GB of free hard disk space available for Office installation.
- A CD-ROM drive.
- A keyboard and mouse or other pointing device.
- A 1024 x 768 resolution monitor is recommended.
- Network cards and cabling for local network access.
- Internet access (contact your local network administrator).
- A printer (optional) or an installed printer driver.
- A projection system to display the instructor's computer screen.

Software

- Microsoft® Office Professional Edition 2010
- Microsoft Office Suite Service Pack 1
- Windows XP Professional with Service Pack 2

This course was developed using the Windows XP operating system; however, the manufacturer's documentation states that it will also run on Vista. If you use Vista, you might notice some slight differences when keying the course.

Class Setup

Initial Class Setup

1. Install Windows XP Professional on an empty partition.

    ■ Leave the Administrator password blank.

    ■ For all other installation parameters, use values that are appropriate for your environment (see your local network administrator for details).

2. On Windows XP Professional, disable the Welcome screen. (This step ensures that students will be able to log on as the Administrator regardless of other user accounts that exist on the computer.)

    a. Click **Start** and choose **Control Panel→User Accounts.**

    b. Click **Change The Way Users Log On And Off.**

    c. Uncheck **Use Welcome Screen.**

    d. Click **Apply Options.**

3. For Windows XP Professional, install Service Pack 2. Use the Service Pack installation defaults.

4. On the computer, install a printer driver (a physical print device is optional). Click **Start** and choose **Printers And Faxes.** Under **Printer Tasks,** click **Add A Printer** and follow the prompts.

    If you do not have a physical printer installed, right-click the printer and choose **Pause Printing** to prevent any print error messages.

5. Run the Internet Connection Wizard to set up the Internet connection appropriately for your environment, if you did not do so during installation.

6. Display known file type extensions.

    a. Open Windows Explorer (right-click) **Start** and then choose **Explore.**

    b. Choose **Tools→Folder Options.**

    c. On the **View** tab, in the **Advanced Settings** list box, uncheck **Hide Extensions For Known File Types.**

    d. Click **Apply,** and then click **OK.**

    e. Close Windows Explorer.

7. Log on to the computer as the Administrator user if you have not already done so.

8. Perform a complete installation of Microsoft Office Professional 2010.

9. Install Microsoft Office Suite Service Pack 1.

10. In the **User Name** dialog box, click **OK** to accept the default user name and initials.

11. In the **Microsoft Office 2010 Activation Wizard** dialog box, click **Next** to activate the Office 2010 application.

12. When the activation of Microsoft Office 2010 is complete, click **Close** to close the **Microsoft Office 2010 Activation Wizard** dialog box.

13. In the **User Name** dialog box, click **OK.**

14. In the **Welcome To Microsoft 2010** dialog box, click **Finish.** You must have an active Internet connection in order to complete this step. Select the **Download And Install Updates From Microsoft Update When Available (Recommended)** option so that whenever there is a new update it gets automatically installed in your system.

15. After the Microsoft Update is run, in the **Microsoft Office** dialog box, click **OK.**

16. Minimize the Language Bar, if necessary.

If your book did not come with a CD, please go to **http:// www.elementk.com/ courseware-file-downloads** to download the data files.

17. On the course CD-ROM, open the 084582 folder. Then, open the Data folder. Run the 084582dd.exe self-extracting file located in it. This will install a folder named 084582Data on your C drive. This folder contains all the data files that you will use to complete this course. If your course did not come with a CD, please go to **http:// elementkcourseware.com** to download the data files.

Within each lesson folder, you may find a Solution folder. This folder contains solution files for the lesson's activities and lesson lab, which can be used by students to check their end results.

Customize the Windows Desktop

Customize the Windows desktop to display the My Computer and My Network Places icons on the student and instructor systems:

1. Right-click the desktop and choose **Properties.**

2. Select the **Desktop** tab.

3. Click **Customize Desktop.**

4. In the **Desktop Items** dialog box, check **My Computer** and **My Network Places.**

5. Click **OK** and click **Apply.**

6. Close the **Display Properties** dialog box.

Before Every Class

1. Log on to the computer as the Administrator user.

2. Delete the existing C:\084582Data folder and extract a fresh copy of the course data files from the CD-ROM provided with the course manual or download the data files from **http:// elementkcourseware.com**.

3. In Microsoft Word, reset the **Results Should Be** options in the **Clip Art** task pane to All Media Types.

   a. In the **Clip Art** task pane, display the Results Should Be drop-down list.

   b. Select **All Media Types.**

   c. To clear "money" from the search list, search for "house."

   d. Close the **Clip Art** task pane.

4. Open the **AutoCorrect Options** dialog box, and select and delete the op/OGC Properties entry.

5. Open the **Research Options** dialog box, click **Update/Remove,** and select and remove the Factiva iWorks service.

6. From the **Save** tab of the **Word Options** dialog box, set the default file location to C:\Documents and Settings\Administrator\My Documents.

7. From the **Customize** category of the **Word Options** dialog box, reset the Quick Access toolbar.

8. For the **Proofing** category of the **Word Options** dialog box, uncheck **Show Readability Statistics.**

9. To eliminate any changes students might have inadvertently made to the Normal template, re-create the Normal.dotm template.

    a. Close Word.

    b. Delete C:\Documents and Settings\Administrator\Application Data\Microsoft\ Templates\Normal.dotm.

    c. Re-open Word.

10. If you have a printer driver installed and it has paused while printing, clear all documents from the print queue.

    a. Open the Printers or Printers And Faxes window.

    b. Right-click the printer.

    c. Choose **Cancel All Documents.**

    d. Click **Yes** and close the window.

List of Additional Files

Printed with each activity is a list of files students open to complete that activity. Many activities also require additional files that students do not open, but are needed to support the file(s) students are working with. These supporting files are included with the student data files on the course CD-ROM or data disk. Do not delete these files.

1 | Getting Started with Word 2010

Lesson Time: 1 hour(s), 30 minutes

Lesson Objectives:

In this lesson, you will identify and work with basic Word 2010 tools and features.

You will:

- Identify the components of the Word interface.
- Customize the Word interface.
- Display a document in different views.
- Enter text in a document.
- Save a document.

Introduction

You have used simple electronic text processors to create documents. Microsoft Word 2010, with its streamlined user interface and various tools for document creation and editing, makes the authoring experience relatively easier. In this lesson, you will identify the basic features and tools of Word 2010.

Learning something new starts with learning how to perform the most basic set of tasks. This also applies to working with a new application. Familiarizing yourself with the user interface of Word will help you acquire the fundamental skills needed for creating simple as well as complex documents.

TOPIC A
Identify the Components of the Word Interface

Working with any new application requires you to become familiar with its interface. Similarly, before you start working with Word 2010, you need to be aware of the various components that are available on the interface. In this topic, you will identify the elements of the Word user interface.

While working with new software, you could potentially waste a significant amount of time searching for specific options in the work environment. You can prevent this by familiarizing yourself with the elements of the user interface. This will help you achieve the output that you are seeking when you work with the software.

Microsoft Word 2010

Microsoft Word 2010 is an application that is used to create, revise, and save documents for printing, distribution, or future retrieval. By using the various typing aids and visual tools available in this application, you can make your documents not only accurate, but also attractive. Microsoft Word 2010 is part of the Microsoft Office 2010 suite, which is a collection of services and applications that help you create documents, spreadsheets, presentations, and databases.

Word Documents

Definition:

A *Word document* is an electronic document that is created by using the Microsoft Word application. It is a collection of pages containing information in the form of text, graphics, tables, or charts that is stored in an electronic form on a computer. You can customize document pages to suit your needs. The default file format for a Word 2010 document is the DOCX format.

Example:

Electronic document created using
Microsoft Word

| Page displaying text | Page displaying a graphic | Page displaying tables |

Figure 1-1: Pages from a Word document.

The Word Application Window

The Word 2010 application window displays components that enable you to work effectively and efficiently on your documents.

Figure 1-2: The components of the Word application window.

Window Component	Description
The *title bar*	A bar located at the top of the application window that displays the name of the document that is open in the window.
The *Quick Access toolbar*	A toolbar that is displayed at the top-left corner of the title bar that provides easy access to core commands such as **Save, Undo,** and **Redo.** It can also be positioned below the Ribbon, and can be customized to include other commands, based on the user's preferences and requirements.
The *Ribbon*	A panel displayed below the title bar that provides access to commands in the application. The commands in this panel are organized into different tabs and groups.
The *status bar*	A bar located at the bottom of the application window that displays a number of options relating to the overall document functionality. It also allows you to switch between various document views and zoom in and out of a document. Information on the status bar can be displayed or hidden as desired.
The *scroll bars*	Vertical and horizontal bars located at the extreme right and bottom of the application window, respectively, that allow you to navigate through a document.

The Ribbon

The Ribbon contains a selection of easy-to-browse commands from which you can choose to work on a document. The commands are grouped according to their functionality. Groups are located within a broader functional group called a tab. The Ribbon can also be customized by adding or removing tabs, groups, and commands that are present in each group. You can also minimize the Ribbon to show only the tab names.

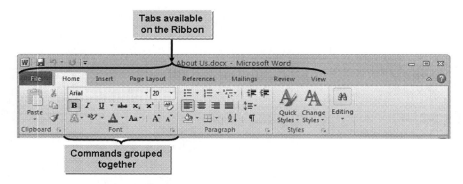

Figure 1-3: *The Home tab of the Ribbon displaying commands in various groups.*

The Ribbon tabs allow you to access commands that perform simple or advanced operations without having to navigate extensively.

Tab	Description
File	Displays the Backstage view with commands that help you perform tasks such as saving, opening, closing, printing, and sharing a document. Using this tab, you can access the **Word Options** dialog box to customize the Word environment. You can also access the Word Help feature.
Home	Contains commonly used commands that enable you to start working with a Word document. It contains functional groups that allow you to format and edit text. The different groups on this tab include **Clipboard, Font, Paragraph, Styles,** and **Editing.**
Insert	Contains commands that enable quick access to different object types such as charts, tables, and pictures that can be added to a document. Groups on this tab include **Pages, Tables, Illustrations, Links, Header & Footer, Text,** and **Symbols.**
Page Layout	Contains commands that are used to customize the pages in a document. By using the commands on this tab, the placement of text and graphics can also be controlled. Groups on this tab include **Themes, Page Setup, Page Background, Paragraph,** and **Arrange.**
References	Contains commands that are used to create references to the content in a document. Groups on this tab include **Table of Contents, Footnotes, Citations & Bibliography, Captions, Index,** and **Table of Authorities.**
Mailings	Contains commands that are used to create documents such as fax, letters, and email that are customized for the recipients. Groups on this tab include **Create, Start Mail Merge, Write & Insert Fields, Preview Results,** and **Finish.**
Review	Contains commands to review and edit the content in a document. Groups on this tab include **Proofing, Comments, Language, Tracking, Changes, Compare,** and **Protect.**
View	Contains various options that enable you to switch between the different document views. Groups on this tab include **Document Views, Show, Zoom, Window,** and **Macros.**

ScreenTips

When you position the mouse pointer over items such as command buttons and other elements in the application window, Word may display a label called a *ScreenTip*. A ScreenTip displays the name of a command and may include a description of the command and the shortcut to access the command. You can use a ScreenTip to identify new application window elements or to distinguish between similar looking buttons.

Dialog Box Launchers

Dialog box launchers are small buttons with downward pointing arrows that occupy the bottom-right corner of certain groups on the Ribbon. They launch dialog boxes or task panes with commands that are specific to the features found in that group. These commands are used to adjust the settings that are not available on the Ribbon.

The Backstage View

The *Backstage view* in Word 2010 is the interface that is displayed when you select the **File** tab. It contains a series of tabs that group similar commands, and displays the compatibility, permissions, and version information about a Word document. It simplifies access to the features in Word and lets you save, share, print, and publish documents with a few mouse clicks.

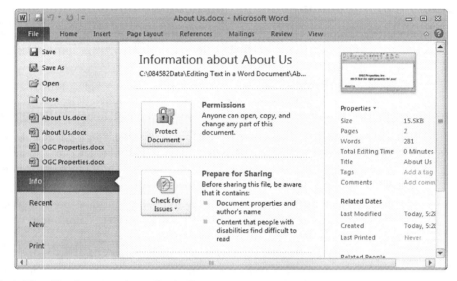

Figure 1-4: *The Backstage view displaying options on the File tab.*

Task Panes

A *task pane* is a small window that is displayed within the Word environment. It provides feature-specific options and commands. A task pane can be resized, moved, and kept open while working on a document. The options in a task pane depend upon the content in a document. Task panes can be opened either by using specific commands on the Ribbon or from within other task panes.

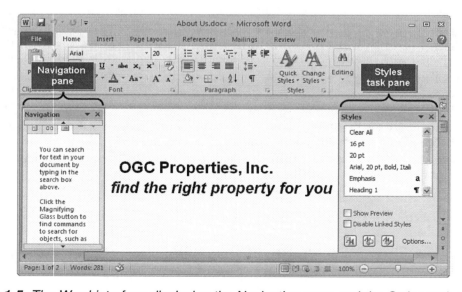

Figure 1-5: *The Word interface displaying the Navigation pane and the Styles task pane.*

Galleries

A *gallery* is a repository for elements that belong to the same category. It acts as a central location for accessing the various styles and appearance settings of an object. Galleries provide you with a set of visual choices to enhance the look and feel of elements while working on a document. Word provides galleries for various options such as styles, tables, shapes, and WordArt. Galleries enable you to choose from any of the preset formats and styles to quickly alter an object in a document. Some galleries are also accessible from shortcut menus, giving you quick access to gallery options. Galleries are arranged either on a grid or in a menu-like layout.

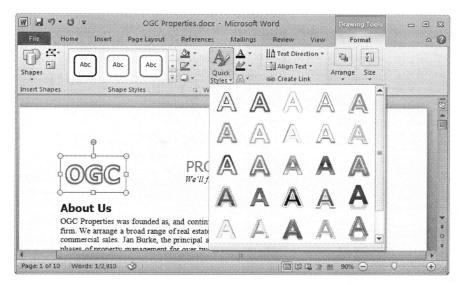

Figure 1-6: *The Quick Styles gallery displaying the various styles.*

Word Help

The *Word Help* feature is a repository of information about the functionality of various features of Microsoft Word 2010. The Word Help window provides you with a quick and easy way to find answers to Word-related queries, online or offline. You can also search for information by browsing through the available links or by performing keyword-based searches. You can access the Word help feature by pressing **F1** or clicking the **Microsoft Word Help** button.

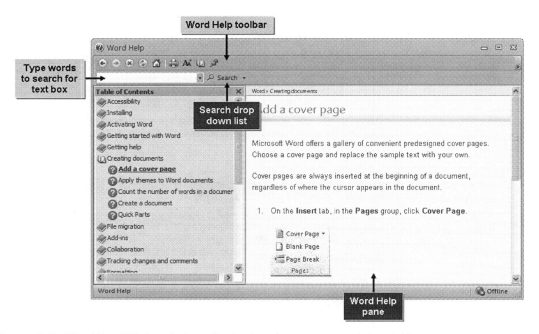

Figure 1-7: *The Word Help window displaying the contents of the Add a cover page.*

The Word Help window provides you with a number of components that allow you to find answers to all your Word-related queries.

Component	Description
The Word Help toolbar	Allows you to access the navigation, print, and format commands.
The **Type words to search for** text box	Allows you to type the keyword on which you need to search for information. Search terms that were used previously can be selected from the **Type words to search for** drop-down list.
The **Search** drop-down list	Allows you to search Word Help for information from online or offline content with the help of the options provided, based on the chosen criterion.
The **Word Help** pane	Displays the topics available in Word Help in a tabular form. You can navigate to a topic and display its content in the pane by clicking the corresponding link.

Word Help Toolbar Options
The buttons on the **Word Help** toolbar enable you to navigate through Word Help.

Button	Used To
Back	Navigate to the page that was previously accessed.
Forward	Navigate to the next page. This button is enabled only after the **Back** button has been used.
Stop	Stop the search that is in progress.
Refresh	Refresh the page that is displayed.
Home	Display the **Home** page of Word Help.

Button	Used To
Print	Print a help page with specific options.
Change Font Size	Increase or decrease the font size of the text in a help topic.
Show Table of Contents	Display the task pane that contains the table of contents of Word Help.
Keep On Top/Not On Top	Position the Word Help window on top of the other windows of Microsoft Word or position other Word windows on top of the Help window. By clicking the **Keep On Top** button, you can toggle to the **Not On Top** button.

Areas of Search

In Word Help, you can specify the area of search to narrow down the search results. Areas of search can be either online or offline.

Area of Search	Provides
All Word	Information about the searched keyword from the built-in help resources and takes you to the Office online website, if required.
Word Help	Information about the searched keyword from the built-in help resources and the Office online website, but does not take you to the Office online website.
Word Templates	Sample templates that are available in the Office online website.
Word Training	Sample training information from the Office online website.
Developer Reference	Programming tasks, samples, and references to create customized solutions.

ACTIVITY 1-1

Identifying the Elements of the Word User Interface

Scenario:

Our Global Company (OGC) is a conglomerate corporation that offers a wide variety of products and services with branches throughout the world. The real estate division of the company is OGC Properties. You are a new recruit in OGC Properties. Your company has just purchased and installed the Microsoft Word 2010 application. Your manager expects you to use this software to create documents. Because you will be frequently working with Word, you need to spend some time to identify the elements of the user interface.

1.   Examine the Backstage view.

   a.   Choose **Start→All Programs→Microsoft Office→Microsoft Word 2010.**

   b.   In the **User Name** dialog box, click **OK.**

   c.   In the Document1 - Microsoft Word window, select the **File** tab to display the Backstage view.

   d.   Observe the various options available in the Backstage view and select the **Home** tab to close the Backstage view.

2.   Examine the groups on the Ribbon.

   a.   Observe that the **Home** tab includes various groups such as **Clipboard, Font, Paragraph, Styles,** and **Editing.**

   b.   Select the **Insert** tab to view the groups available in it.

   c.   On the Ribbon, select the other tabs to view the groups available on the respective tabs.

3.   View the options in the **Page Setup** dialog box.

   a.   Select the **Page Layout** tab, and in the **Page Setup** group, at the bottom-right corner, click the **Page Setup** dialog box launcher.

   b.   Observe the options in the **Page Setup** dialog box and click **Cancel** to close the dialog box.

4.   Display the Page Color gallery.

a. On the **Page Layout** tab, in the **Page Background** group, click the **Page Color** drop-down arrow to display the Page Color gallery.

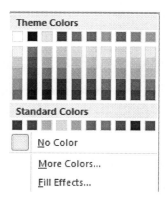

b. Click the drop-down arrow again to close the gallery.

5. Display a task pane.

a. Select the **Home** tab, and in the **Styles** group, click the **Styles** dialog box launcher.

b. Observe that the **Styles** task pane is displayed with various Word style options that are available.

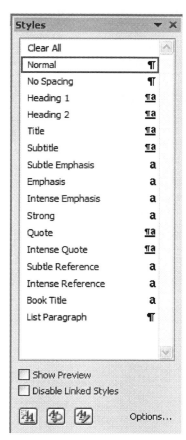

    c.   In the **Styles** task pane, at the top-right corner, click the **Close** button to close the task pane.

6.   Display the Word Help window.

    a.   On the Ribbon, at the top-right corner, click the **Microsoft Word Help** button.

    b.   In the Word Help window, at the top-right corner, click the **Maximize** button.

7.   View help information.

    a.   In the Word Help window, in the **Word Help and How to** pane, in the **Browse Word Help** section, click the **Getting started with Word** link.

    b.   In the **Getting started with Word** pane, click the **Introducing the Backstage view** link.

    c.   Observe that information about the Backstage view in Word is displayed.

8.   Keep the Word Help window on top of the open Word window.

    a.   In the Word Help window, on the title bar, click the **Restore Down** button to restore the Word Help window to its original state.

    b.   In the Word Help window, on the Word Help toolbar, place the mouse pointer over the **Keep On Top** button and observe that it is set as the default option.

    c.   Click anywhere in the Word window.

    d.   Observe that the Word Help window stays on top, and at the top-right corner of the window, click the **Close** button to close the window.

    e.   Select the **File** tab and choose **Close.**

TOPIC B

Customize the Word Interface

You explored the Word user interface. If the default display and arrangement of the interface elements are not appropriate to your liking or workflow, Word provides options to personalize the interface to suit individual requirements. In this topic, you will customize the Word environment.

When you start working with new software, the interface by default may not display all the options that you require, or it may be cluttered with options that you may not require at all. This will slow you down and make working a cumbersome process. By customizing the environment, you will be able to display those options that you need for the current workflow.

The Word Options Dialog Box

The *Word Options dialog box* contains a series of tabs, each of which contains commands that allow you to customize the Word environment.

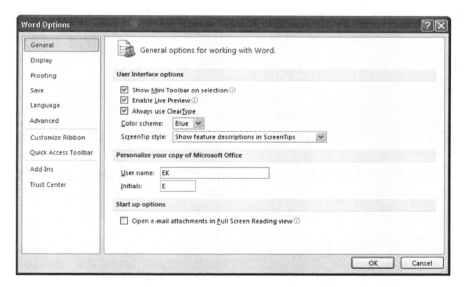

Figure 1-8: The Word Options dialog box displaying the options on the General tab.

Tab	Description
General	Allows you to personalize the work environment by setting the color scheme, user name, and start-up options. It also allows you to enable the Live Preview feature.
Display	Allows you to modify how text content is displayed on screen and in the print version. You can opt to show or hide certain page elements such as highlighter marks and formatting marks.
Proofing	Enables you to specify how Word should correct and format text that you type. You can set the auto-correction settings and ensure that Word corrects all the spelling and grammatical errors. You can also ensure that Word ignores certain words or errors in a document.

Tab	Description
Save	Enables you to specify the customization options for saving documents. Depending on how often you want to save the backup information of your documents, you can specify the frequency at which a document will be auto saved. You can also change the locations of where these drafts will be saved.
Language	Allows you to modify the Word language preferences.
Advanced	Enables you to specify options for editing, copying, pasting, displaying, printing, saving, and writing content. It also provides advanced options needed to work with Word.
Customize Ribbon	Enables you to customize the Ribbon. Using the options on this tab, you can select the additional tabs, groups, and commands that you want to display on the Ribbon.
Quick Access Toolbar	Enables you to customize the Quick Access toolbar. Using the options on this tab, you can select the commands that you want to add to the Quick Access toolbar. You can also opt to position the Quick Access toolbar below the Ribbon.
Add-Ins	Allows you to manage Office add-ins if you are using extensions to enhance Office applications. Extensions are add-ins that introduce new functionality to an application. Many add-ins are installed with Office 2010.
Trust Center	Allows you to secure the system and documents. Using the **Advanced Trust Center Settings** button on this tab, you can set the security measures that are needed to secure a document.

How to Customize the Word Interface

Procedure Reference: Customize the Quick Access Toolbar Using the Word Options Dialog Box

To customize the Quick Access toolbar using the **Word Options** dialog box:

1. Display the **Word Options** dialog box.
    *   Select the **File** tab and choose **Options** or;
    *   On the Quick Access toolbar, from the **Customize Quick Access Toolbar** menu, choose **More Commands** or;
    *   On the Ribbon, right-click and select **Customize Quick Access Toolbar.**
2. In the **Word Options** dialog box, select the **Quick Access Toolbar** tab.
3. From the **Choose commands from** drop-down list, select a category from which a command is to be added to the Quick Access toolbar.
4. In the **Choose commands from** list box, select a command and click **Add** to add the command to the Quick Access toolbar.
5. If necessary, in the **Customize Quick Access Toolbar** list box, select a command and click **Remove** to remove the command from the Quick Access toolbar.
6. Position the commands on the Quick Access toolbar.
    *   In the **Customize Quick Access Toolbar** list box, select a command and click the **Move Up** button to move the command up one level.
    *   In the **Customize Quick Access Toolbar** list box, select a command and click the **Move Down** button to move the command down one level.
    *   In the **Customize Quick Access Toolbar** list box, select a command and drag it above or below another command to specify its position on the Quick Access toolbar.

7. If necessary, add or remove more commands from the **Customize Quick Access Toolbar** list box.

8. If necessary, check or uncheck the **Show Quick Access Toolbar below the Ribbon** check box to place the Quick Access toolbar below or above the Ribbon.

 You can also reposition the Quick Access toolbar below the Ribbon by selecting **Show Below The Ribbon** from the **Customize Quick Access Toolbar** menu.

9. Click **OK** to close the **Word Options** dialog box.

Procedure Reference: Add a Command or Group from the Ribbon to the Quick Access Toolbar

To add a command or group from the Ribbon to the Quick Access toolbar:

1. On the Ribbon, select the tab that has the desired command or group.

2. Right-click the command or group and choose **Add to Quick Access Toolbar.**

 You can add any number of groups to the Quick Access toolbar. However, the Ribbon itself cannot be added to the Quick Access toolbar.

3. If necessary, on the Quick Access toolbar, click the group to verify that all the commands in the group have been added.

Procedure Reference: Add a Command to the Quick Access Toolbar Using the Customize Quick Access Toolbar Menu

To add a command to the Quick Access toolbar using the **Customize Quick Access Toolbar** menu:

1. On the Quick Access toolbar, click the **Customize Quick Access Toolbar** drop-down arrow.

2. From the **Customize Quick Access Toolbar** menu, choose a command to include it on the Quick Access toolbar.

 If you choose a command that is already displayed on the Quick Access toolbar, it will be removed from the Quick Access toolbar.

Procedure Reference: Customize the Status Bar

To customize the status bar:

1. In the Word application, right-click the status bar.

2. From the displayed menu, choose the required options to be added to or removed from the status bar.

 On the menu, when you choose an option, a check mark is displayed to its left to indicate that the selected option will be displayed on the status bar. Choosing the desired option again hides it.

3. Click away from the menu to close it.

Minimizing the Ribbon

Although it is not possible to move or hide the Ribbon, you can minimize it so that more space will be available in the work area. You can double-click the active tab on the Ribbon, click the **Minimize The Ribbon** button present at the top-right corner of the Ribbon, or press **Ctrl+F1** to minimize the Ribbon. The interface will display only the tabs, while the corresponding groups and galleries will be hidden. To restore the Ribbon, select any of the tabs.

Procedure Reference: Create a Ribbon Tab and a Group with Commands

To create a Ribbon tab and a group with commands:

1. Display the **Word Options** dialog box.
2. In the **Word Options** dialog box, select the **Customize Ribbon** tab.
3. In the **Customize the Ribbon** list box, check or uncheck the check boxes for the tabs to show or hide them on the Ribbon.
4. Below the **Customize the Ribbon** list box, click **New Tab** to create a tab with a group.
5. If necessary, below the **Customize the Ribbon** list box, click **New Group** to create a group.
6. Rename a tab or a group.
   a. In the **Customize the Ribbon** list box, select a tab or a group that you want to rename.
   b. Display the **Rename** dialog box.
      • Below the **Customize the Ribbon** list box, click **Rename** or;
      • Right-click the tab or group and choose **Rename.**
   c. In the **Rename** dialog box, type a new name and click **OK.**
7. Add commands to a group.
   a. From the **Choose commands from** drop-down list, select a category from which you want to choose commands.
   b. In the **Choose commands from** list box, select a command that you want to add to the group.
   c. In the **Customize the Ribbon** list box, select a tab and group to which you want to add the command.
   d. Click **Add** to add the selected command.
8. If necessary, in the **Customize the Ribbon** list box, select a command and click **Remove** to remove a command from the group.
9. If necessary, create more tabs and groups and add commands to them.
10. In the **Word Options** dialog box, click **OK** to add the new tab with the chosen commands to the Ribbon.

ACTIVITY 1-2
Customizing the Word User Interface

Scenario:

As you start working with Word, you realize that there are a few commands that you will use frequently. Adding these commands to the Quick Access toolbar will increase your efficiency. You also notice that paragraph alignment commands will be used often when working with Word documents. You want to customize the Ribbon by adding a new tab with a few commands to make it easier for you to use these commands in your document. You also notice that the status bar displays some information which you will not require. In addition, you want to familiarize yourself with changing the information that can be displayed on the status bar.

---

1. Add commands to the Quick Access toolbar.

    a. On the Quick Access toolbar, click the **Customize Quick Access Toolbar** drop-down arrow.

    b. From the **Customize Quick Access Toolbar** menu, choose **Open** to add the **Open** command to the Quick Access toolbar.

    c. Observe that the **Open** button is added to the **Quick Access Toolbar.** Select the **File** tab and choose **Options.**

    d. In the **Word Options** dialog box, select the **Quick Access Toolbar** tab.

    e. In the **Choose commands from** list box, scroll down, and select **New.**

    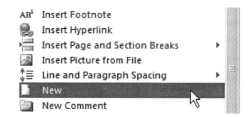

    f. Click **Add** to add the **New** command to the Quick Access toolbar.

    g. From the **Choose commands from** drop-down list, select **File Tab.**

    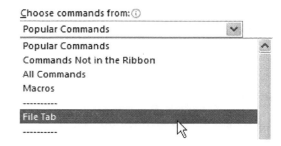

h. In the **Choose commands from** list box, select **Close** and click **Add** to add the command to the Quick Access toolbar.

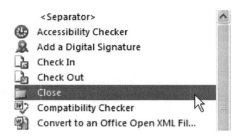

i. Click **OK** to close the **Word Options** dialog box.

j. Observe that the **New** and **Close** buttons are displayed on the Quick Access toolbar.

2. Add the **Paragraph** group to the Quick Access toolbar.

a. On the **Home** tab, in the **Paragraph** group, right-click **Paragraph** and choose **Add to Quick Access Toolbar.**

b. On the Quick Access toolbar, click the **Paragraph** button to open the **Paragraph** group.

c. Observe that all the **Paragraph** group options are now accessible from the Quick Access toolbar and click the **Paragraph** button again to hide the paragraph options.

3. Customize the status bar.

a. On the status bar, right-click anywhere to view the **Customize Status Bar** menu.

b. From the **Customize Status Bar** menu, choose **Section.**

c. Observe that a check mark is displayed next to **Section,** indicating that section information will be displayed on the status bar.

| ✓ | Section | ⇲ | 1 |

d. From the **Customize Status Bar** menu, choose **Line Number**

| ✓ | Line Number | ⇲ | 1 |

and **Column**

| ✓ | Column | ⇲ | 1 |

to display information on line numbers and column numbers on the status bar.

e. Choose **Word Count**

| | Word Count ⇲ | 0 |

to remove the number of information about number of words in the selection or document from the status bar.

f. Click away from the **Customize Status Bar** menu to close the menu.

4. Add a new tab to the Ribbon.

a. Select the **File** tab and choose **Options.**

| 🗐 Options | ⇲ |

b. In the **Word Options** dialog box, select the **Customize Ribbon** tab.

c. In the right pane, in the **Customize the Ribbon** list box, select **View.**

```
Main Tabs
☐ ☑ Home
      ⊞ Clipboard
      ⊞ Font
      ⊞ Paragraph
      ⊞ Styles
      ⊞ Editing
 ⊞ ☑ Insert
 ⊞ ☑ Page Layout
 ⊞ ☑ References
 ⊞ ☑ Mailings
 ⊞ ☑ Review
 ⊞ ☑ View
 ⊞ ☐ Developer
 ⊞ ☑ Add-Ins
 ⊞ ☑ Blog Post
 ⊞ ☑ Insert (Blog Post)
 ⊞ ☑ Outlining
 ⊞ ☑ Background Removal
```

d. Below the **Customize the Ribbon** list box, click **New Tab.**

e. Observe that in the **Customize the Ribbon** list box, **New Tab (Custom)** and **New Group (Custom)** are displayed.

f. Select **New Tab (Custom)** and click **Rename** [Rename...] to rename the tab.

g. In the **Rename** dialog box, in the **Display name** text box, type *Favorites* and click **OK.**

5. Rename the default group and add commands to it.

a. In the **Customize the Ribbon** list box, select **New Group (Custom)** and click **Rename.**

b. In the **Rename** dialog box, in the **Display name** text box, type *My Favorite Commands* and click **OK.**

c. From the **Choose commands from** drop-down list, select **Commands not in the Ribbon.**

d. In the **Choose commands from** list box, select **All Caps** [ᵃA All Caps] and click **Add.**

e. Scroll down and select **AutoCorrect Days** [AutoCorrect Days] and click **Add.**

f. Click **OK** to exit the **Word Options** dialog box.

g. On the Ribbon, select the **Favorites** tab to display the commands that were added to the newly created group.

TOPIC C
Display a Document in Different Views

You customized the Word environment to match your requirements. Before you start working on a document, you may need to choose an appropriate view in which the document should be displayed. In this topic, you will view a document in different views.

Imagine that you are asked to view a report that is difficult to read in the default view of Word. Word 2010 provides options to view the document in different views and display it in a view that best suits your requirements. Each view has its own use, and understanding the purpose of each document view will help you work more effectively with your document.

Word Templates

A *Word template* is a predefined Word document that is used as a basis for creating other documents or templates. Every document in Word is based on a template. Word templates provide the basic structure, layout, formatting, and special characteristics for a document by storing styles and other document elements, such as the default document font, page layout settings, and boilerplate text. Word templates are of two types: *document templates,* which are used to create specific document types, and *global templates,* which store settings that are available to all open documents.

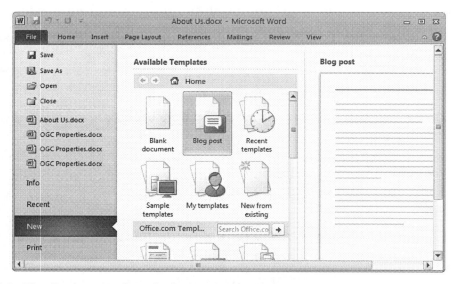

Figure 1-9: *The Backstage view displaying the available templates and a preview of the Blog post template.*

Document Views

The status bar contains options that enable you to display a Word document in different views.

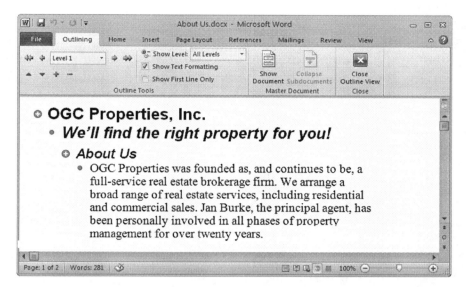

Figure 1-10: *A document displayed in the outline view.*

Document	Description
Print Layout	Allows you to view a document as it will appear when printed. All sections such as tables, text, and graphics will be displayed in their correct positions in the document.
Full Screen Reading	Allows you to view a document on the entire screen. This view is ideal for viewing multiple pages at a time.
Web Layout	Allows you to view a document as it will be displayed in a web browser. In this view, the entire document is displayed on a single page, with tables and text wrapping to fit in the window.
Outline	Allows you to view a document as an outline, where the document is displayed with bullets and plus signs, which can be expanded or collapsed to display or hide the subordinate levels of text.
Draft	Allows you to view a document as a draft. In this view, the document is displayed without pictures and layouts to ensure that the focus is only on the text.

 In the Outline view, the **Outlining** tab is displayed on the Ribbon. Using this tab, you can manipulate the existing outline by changing the heading or body text of the chosen content and then formatting it.

Window Views

The **Window** group on the **View** tab contains various options that allow you to manipulate the appearance of Word documents.

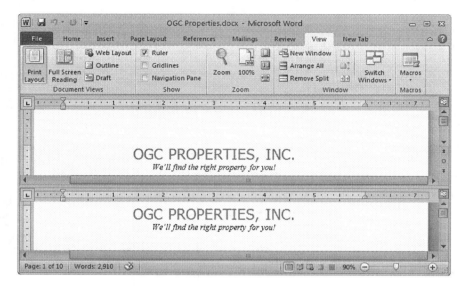

Figure 1-11: *A document displayed in split view.*

Option	Description
New Window	Opens the current document in a new window.
Arrange All	Arranges open document windows side-by-side on the screen.
Split	Splits a window into multiple panes to view different sections of a document.
View Side by Side	Views two open document windows side-by-side.
Synchronous Scrolling	Synchronizes the scrolling of two documents that are displayed side-by-side so that they can be scrolled together. This option is available only when the **View Side by Side** option is enabled.
Reset Window Position	Resets open windows so that both document windows occupy 50% of the screen. This option is available only when the **View Side by Side** option is enabled.
Switch Windows	Switches to another open document window.

Zoom Options

The options on the status bar allow you to set the magnification level of a document. Zoom options can also be set on the Ribbon and in the **Zoom** dialog box.

Option	Description
Zoom	Displays the **Zoom** dialog box in which you can set the magnification level. This option is accessible from the status bar as well as the **Zoom** group on the **View** tab of the Ribbon.
100%	Allows you to set the magnification level to 100%.
One Page	Allows you to magnify the document so that an entire page is displayed within the window.
Two Pages	Allows you to magnify the document so that two pages are displayed within the window.
Page Width	Allows you to magnify the document so that the page width fits the width of the window.
Zoom Slider	Comprises the **Zoom In** and **Zoom Out** buttons on either side of the **Zoom Slider** on the status bar. You can drag the slider to either side or click the zoom buttons to change the magnification level.

How to Display a Document in Different Views

Procedure Reference: Open a Word Document

To open a word document:

1. Select the **File** tab and choose **Open.**
2. In the **Open** dialog box, navigate to the desired location, select a file, and click **Open.**

Procedure Reference: Open a Sample Template

To open a sample template:

1. Select the **File** tab and choose **New.**
2. In the Backstage view, in the **Available Templates** pane, select **Sample templates.**
3. On the **Sample templates** page, select a template and click **Create.**

Procedure Reference: Find Templates on the Web

To find templates on the web:

1. Select the **File** tab, and choose **New.**
2. On the **Available Templates** page, in the **Office.com Templates** search box, enter a keyword to identify the type of template you require, and then click **Start searching** to search for templates on the web.

Procedure Reference: Display a Document in Different Document Views

To display a document in different document views:

1. Open a document from a template or an existing document.

2. Select a document view.

   - On the status bar, click a view button to view the document in the corresponding view or;

   - On the **View** tab, in the **Document Views** group, select a view.

 When you open a document in the Full Screen Reading or Outline view, you should close the view before displaying the document in another view.

Procedure Reference: Display a Document in Different Window Views

To display a document in different window views:

1. Open a document from a template or an existing document.

2. On the **View** tab, in the **Window** group, select a view.

Switching Between Documents

You can switch between open documents using a number of techniques.

   - On the **View** tab, in the **Window** group, choose **Switch Windows** to display the list of documents that is open and to select the document that you want to display.

   - Press **Ctrl+F6** to switch between open Word documents.

   - Press **Alt+Tab** to switch between all the open documents.

   - Click the appropriate button on the Windows taskbar.

Procedure Reference: Magnify a Document Using the Zoom Options

To magnify a document using the zoom options:

1. Open a document with text in one or more pages.

2. On the **View** tab, in the **Zoom** group, change the zoom levels.

   - Click **Zoom,** and in the **Zoom** dialog box, set a magnification level.

   - Click **100%** to set the magnification level to 100%.

   - Click **One Page** to view an entire page within the window.

   - Click **Two Pages** to view two pages within the window.

   - Click **Page Width** to expand the page to the width of the window.

3. If necessary, on the status bar, move the Zoom slider to magnify the document to the desired level.

ACTIVITY 1-3
Displaying a Document in Different View Modes

Scenario:

Before you start working on a document, you want to determine the best view in which to work on it. You decide to check out the different view modes using a sample template so that you can identify the one that best suits your requirements.

1. Open a sample template.

   a. Select the **File** tab, and in the Backstage view, in the **Available Templates** pane, select **Sample templates**.

   Sample
   templates

   b. On the **Sample templates** pane, scroll down, select **Essential Report,** and click **Create.**

2. View the document in different views.

   a. Select the **View** tab, and in the **Document Views** group, click the **Web Layout** button to switch to the Web Layout view.

   b. Click the **Outline** button to switch to the Outline view.

   c. On the **Outlining** tab, in the **Close** group, click **Close Outline View** to close the Outline view.

   d. In the **Navigation Pane** at the top-right corner, click the **Close** button.

   e. On the status bar, click the **Zoom In** button to magnify the document to 110%, and click the **Zoom Out** button to view the document in the default magnification.

3. Display the document in different window modes.

a. Select the **View** tab, and in the **Window** group, click **Split.**

b. Click the document at the vertical center to split the document window into two sections.

c. In the bottom pane, scroll down to display the text " [TYPE THE DOCUMENT TITLE]."

d. On the **View** tab, in the **Window** group, click **New Window** to display the currently open document in another window.

e. Select the **View** tab, and in the **Window** group, click **View Side by Side** to view the open documents side by side.

f. In the right window, on the Quick Access toolbar, click **Close** to close both the windows.

g. In the **Microsoft Word** message box, click **Don't Save** to close the document without saving the changes.

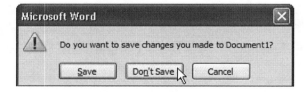

TOPIC D

Enter Text in a Document

You displayed a document in different views. You will, however, find each view more useful when you have suitable content in a document. In this topic, you will create a basic Word document by entering text in it.

Word is a powerful word processor used to create documents that primarily use text to convey information. You need to be familiar with the process of entering text in a document before adding more advanced features such as formatting.

Default Typing Options

Word provides you with various typing options such as *Word Wrap, AutoCorrect, Check spelling and grammar as you type,* and *Smart tags* that help you enter text neatly, quickly, and accurately.

Option	Description
Word Wrap	Automatically wraps a long line of text to the beginning of the next line so that you can continue typing. There is no need to manually end each line of text by pressing **Enter** when you get close to the right margin.
AutoCorrect	Fixes common typographical errors, misspelled words, and incorrect capitalization.
Check spelling and grammar as you type	Displays a wavy red or wavy green line below text that Word considers a spelling or grammar error, respectively. You can right-click the underlined item and Word will suggest corrections for you.
Smart tags	Allows you to perform specific action on data, such as names and dates, that Word recognizes when typed and applies smart tags to them.

The AutoCorrect Options Button

The **AutoCorrect Options** button is displayed below a letter or word that is modified by using the AutoCorrect feature. This button opens a list that provides options to undo automatic corrections, stop particular automatic corrections, or modify the AutoCorrect options by using the **AutoCorrect** dialog box.

Formatting Marks

Formatting marks are non-printable characters that are displayed in the text area to indicate the location of invisible formatting elements such as spaces, paragraph breaks, tabs, and line breaks. By clicking the **Show/Hide** button on the **Home** tab, you can turn the formatting marks on or off.

Line Breaks

A *line break* is a formatting element that is used to end a line before it wraps to the next line, but without starting a new paragraph. You can insert a line break by pressing **Shift+Enter.** The benefit of using a line break within a paragraph, rather than pressing **Enter** to start a new paragraph, is that the new line following the break remains a part of the original paragraph and shares that paragraph's properties.

How to Enter Text in a Document

Procedure Reference: Open an Existing Word Document

To open an existing Word document:

1. Select the **File** tab and choose **Open.**
2. In the **Open** dialog box, navigate to the location where the file is located, select the file, and click **Open.**

Procedure Reference: Open a Blank Word Document

To open a blank Word document:

1. Select the **File** tab and choose **New.**
2. In the **Available Templates** pane, verify that **Blank document** is selected and click **Create.**

Procedure Reference: Enter Text in a Document

To enter text in a document:

1. Open a Word document.
2. If necessary, click at a desired position within the existing content to place the insertion point.
3. Type to add text in the document.
4. If necessary, delete text in the document.
   - Press **Backspace** to delete one character to the left.
   - Press **Delete** to delete one character to the right.
   - Position the mouse pointer at the beginning of the blank line and press **Delete** to delete the blank line.
5. If necessary, press **Enter** to end a paragraph or to create a blank line between paragraphs.
6. If necessary, on the **Home** tab, in the **Paragraph** group, click the **Show/Hide** button, which is the first button from the right in the first row to display the formatting marks.

ACTIVITY 1-4
Entering Text in a Document

Scenario:

You need to draft a document containing information about OGC Properties. You decide to use Word to create the document with the required information.

---

1. Open a blank document.

    a. Select the **File** tab and verify that the option **New** is selected.

    b. In the Backstage view, in the **Available Templates** section, verify that **Blank document** is selected and click **Create.**

    Create

---

2. Type text in the document.

    a. On the **Home** tab, in the **Paragraph** group, click the **Show/Hide** [¶] button to turn on the display of formatting marks.

    b. Type *OGC Properties, Inc.* Then, press **Enter.**

    c. Type *We'll find the right property for you!* and press **Enter.**

    d. Press **Enter** to add a blank line.

    e. Type *About Us* and press **Enter.**

    f. Type *OGC Properties was founded as, and continues to be, a full-service real estate brokerage company. We arrange a wide*

    g. Observe that as you type, the text automatically wraps at the right edge of the document to flow into the next line.

---

3. Replace the word "wide" with "broad" and continue typing text.

    a. Press **Backspace** four times to delete the word "wide."

    b. Type *broad*

    c. Press the **Spacebar** and type *range of real estate services, including residential and commercial sales.*

    d. Press the **Spacebar** and type *Jan Burke, the principal agent, has been personally involved in all the phases of property management for over twenty years.*

---

4. Check the functionality of the AutoCorrect feature.

a. Press the **Spacebar** and type *Tihs* to start the next sentence.

b. Press the **Spacebar.**

c. Observe that the misspelled word is automatically corrected to "This."

d. Move the mouse pointer below the word "This" to display the **AutoCorrect Options**  button and click it.

e. From the **AutoCorrect Options** drop-down list, select **Control AutoCorrect Options.**

f. In the **AutoCorrect: English (U.S.)** dialog box, verify that the **Replace text as you type** check box is checked and in the **Replace text as you type** list box, scroll down.

g. Verify that there is an option to convert "Tihs" to "This."

h. Click **Cancel** to close the **AutoCorrect: English (U.S.)** dialog box.

i. In the document, type *experience includes: historic preservation, restoration, leasing and sales management, and consulting for developers on issues ranging from planning to final marketing.*

j. Press **Enter** to move the insertion point to the next line.

TOPIC E

Save a Document

You entered text in a document. You may want to store this document for future reference. In this topic, you will save a document.

Working on an important document for hours will be an exercise in futility if you cannot store it and retrieve it for future use. Saving a document will ensure that the contents of the document are preserved for future use.

Save Options

Word enables you to save the content of a document using two commands: **Save** and **Save As.** The *Save command* is used to save a newly created document, or to save the changes made to an existing document. While saving a file for the first time, the **Save As** dialog box that prompts the user to specify a file name and the location in which to save the file is displayed. The *Save As command* is used to save an existing document with a new file name or file extension, or in a new location. Additionally, it provides options to save a copy of a file as a template in the Word 97-2003 file format, or to publish it as a PDF or XPS file.

Save vs. Save As

The **Save** command overwrites an existing document with the same name in the same location, whereas the **Save As** command allows you to change the name of the file, the location in which the file needs to be stored, and the file type.

Word 2010 File Formats

Word 2010 files are saved in the eXtensible Markup Language (XML) file format. The Word XML format is a compact and robust file format that enables easy integration of Word documents with other applications and platforms. Word 2010 also supports a number of other file formats.

File Format	*Description*
Word Document (.docx)	The default file format in which all Word 2010 documents are saved.
Word Macro-Enabled Document (.docm)	The basic XML file format that can store VBA macro code. Macros are sets of Word commands and instructions grouped as a single command. A VBA helps in modifying these macros.
Word 97–2003 Document (.doc)	The file format that is used to save documents in the 97–2003 version of Word. It is also used to save documents in the Word 6.0/95 format.
Word Template (.dotx)	The default format for a Word template. It is used for saving document styles and formatting.
Word Macro-Enabled Template (.dotm)	The default format for a Word macro-enabled template. Microsoft Office Word 2010 stores macro code for use with other Word documents. By default, documents are saved as .docx files even when created from a Word 2010 XML macro-enabled template.

File Format	Description
Word 97–2003 Template (.dot)	The file format that enables you to save a Word template in the 97–2003 version.
Portable Document Format (.pdf)	The file format that enables you to save a Word document in the Adobe Portable Document Format (PDF).

Advantages of the XML File Format

Versions of Word before 2007 used the DOC file format as the default file format. The XML based DOCX file format provides several improvements to the DOC file format that are useful for end users.

Feature	Advantage
Smaller file size	The XML file formats use file compression to reduce file sizes by as much as 75%. These file formats reduce the disk space that is required to store files, as well as the bandwidth used to share documents across networks.
Improved information recovery	The files saved in these formats are modularly structured. The different data components in a file are stored separately. Therefore, a file can be opened even if a component within the file is damaged or corrupted.
Easier detection of documents with macros	The file formats with their distinct extensions make it easier to distinguish files that contain macros from those that do not. File extensions ending with 'x' cannot contain VBA macros or ActiveX controls, whereas files ending with 'm' can.
Easier integration and interoperability of information	Information created within the Office applications can be easily used by other applications, across various platforms.

The Compatibility Checker Feature

The *Compatibility Checker feature* in Word 2010 allows you to check different document formats for compatibility when they are saved in an earlier version of Word.

Compatibility Method	Description
Convert a document to an earlier version	You can use the **Convert** option to convert a document saved in an earlier version of Word to the Word 2010 file format.
Save as an earlier version	You can save a document that is saved in the DOCX format, in a file format that is compatible with earlier versions of Word. In the **Save As** dialog box, select the document type for the appropriate version of Word.
Check compatibility	You can use the **Microsoft Word Compatibility Checker** dialog box to check for any compatibility issue in a document.

Compatibility Mode

Word 2010 allows you to work with documents created in previous versions of Word in the Compatibility mode. Working in this mode disables some of the new features of the present version, so that a document created in the new version can be viewed without any hassles in an older version. If a document is viewed in compatibility mode, a visual cue is added on the title bar indicating that it is being viewed as a document in an older version.

The AutoSave Feature

The *AutoSave* feature in Word 2010 automatically saves copies of a document every ten minutes, by default. The options to change the default autosave time are available in the **Word Options** dialog box. You can also set options to save the document in a specific format, retain the last autosaved version of the document that is closed without saving, and set the location where the file will be saved.

How to Save a Document

Procedure Reference: Save a Document Using the Save As Command

To save a document using the **Save As** command:

1. Select the **File** tab and choose **Save As** to display the **Save As** dialog box.
2. In the **Save As** dialog box, set the save options.
    *   Navigate to the location where you want to save the document.
    *   From the **Save as type** drop-down list, select the desired file format.
    *   In the **File name** text box, type a name for the file.
3. Click **Save.**

Procedure Reference: Change File Types

To change file types:

1. Select the **File** tab, and choose **Save & Send.**
2. In the **File Types** section, select **Change File Type.**
3. In the **Document File Types** section or **Other File Types** section, select the desired file type.
    *   Select **Document (*.docx)** to save the document with a different name in the DOCX format.
    *   Select **Word 97–2003 Document (*.doc)** to save the document in an older version of Word.
    *   Select **OpenDocument Text (*.odt)** to save the document in the Open Office format.
    *   Select **Template (*.dotx)** to save the document as a template.
    *   Select **Plain Text (*.txt)** to save the document in plain text format.
    *   Select **Rich Text Format (*.rtf)** to save the document in rich text format.
    *   Select **Single File Web Page (*.mht,*.mhtml)** to save the document as a web page in a single file or;
    *   Select **Save as Another File Type**, to save the document in a word compatible format.
4. Click **Save As.**

5. In the **Save As** dialog box, in the **File name** text box, enter a name for the file.

6. If necessary, from the **Save as type** drop-down list, select a file format.

7. Click **Save** to save the document.

Procedure Reference: Save Changes to an Existing Document

To save changes to an existing document:

1. Open and modify a document, as required.

2. Save the changes.

   ● Select the **File** tab and choose **Save** or;

   ● On the Quick Access toolbar, click the **Save** button or;

   ● Press **Ctrl+S.**

Procedure Reference: Set the AutoSave Options

To set the AutoSave options:

1. Display the **Word Options** dialog box.

2. Select the **Save** tab.

3. In the **Save documents** section, set the AutoSave options.

   ● In the **Save AutoRecover information every minutes** spin box, specify the frequency at which you want the document to be autosaved.

   ● If necessary, check the **Keep the last autosaved version if I close without saving** check box to enable you to recover a document that you closed without saving.

   ● To the right of the **Autorecover file location** text box, click the **Browse** button and specify a folder to save the autosaved files.

 If you set the AutoSave time beyond the default 10 minutes, and you need to recover the file at the 10th minute, the recovered file will not contain any of the data entered in the last 10 minutes. It is advisable to keep the default or to set a shorter AutoSave time to ensure that you do not lose too much data if there is a problem.

4. Click **OK** to close the **Word Options** dialog box.

Procedure Reference: Create a PDF Document

To create a PDF document:

1. Open the document you want to save in the PDF format.

2. Select the **File** tab, and choose **Save & Send.**

3. In the **File Types** section, click **Create PDF/XPS Document.**

4. In the **Create a PDF/XPS Document** section, click **Create PDF/XPS Document.**

5. In the **Publish as PDF or XPS** dialog box, in the **File name** text box, enter a desired name for the folder.

6. From the **Save as type** drop-down list, select **PDF (*.pdf).**

7. Specify the location where you want to store the document and click **Publish** to create a PDF document.

Procedure Reference: Recover an Unsaved Document

To recover an unsaved document:

1. Select the **File** tab and choose **Recent.**

2. In the Backstage view, in the **Recent Places** section, click **Recover Unsaved Documents** to display the **Open** dialog box.

3. In the **Open** dialog box, select an unsaved document and click **Open.**

4. If necessary, on the **Recovered Unsaved File** message bar, click **Save As** and save the file.

Procedure Reference: Recover a Draft Version

To recover a draft version:

1. Select the **File** tab, and choose **Info.**

2. Open a draft version of the document.

   - In the **Versions** section, select the draft version that you want to open or;

   - Use the **Open** dialog box to open a draft version.

     a. Click the **Manage Versions** drop-down arrow, and select **Recover Unsaved Documents.**

     b. In the **Open** dialog box, select an unsaved document and click **Open.**

Procedure Reference: Delete a Draft Version

To delete a draft version:

1. Select the **File** tab, and choose **Info.**

2. In the **Versions** section, right-click the draft version that you want to delete, and choose **Delete This Version.**

Procedure Reference: Check Compatibility when Saved in Earlier Versions

To check compatibility when you save a file in an earlier version of Word:

1. Open a document, make the necessary changes, and on the **File** tab, choose **Save As.**

2. From the **Save as type** drop-down list, select a desired file format and click **Save.**

3. In the **Microsoft Word Compatibility Checker** dialog box, verify that the features that are not supported in the earlier version are displayed and click **Ok.**

ACTIVITY 1-5
Saving a Document

Before You Begin:

The document created in the previous activity is open.

Scenario:

After typing the information about OGC Properties, you wish to maintain a copy of it for your reference. One of the agents, Tim Jones, has only Word 2003 installed on his computer. Therefore, you also need to create a copy of the document in the Word 2003 file format.

1. Close the document without saving the changes.

     Ensure that the document is open for more than 10 minutes.

    a. Select the **File** tab and choose **Close.**

    b. In the **Microsoft Word** message box, click **Don't save.**

2. Recover the unsaved document.

    a. Select the **File** tab and choose **Recent.**

    b. In the Backstage view, in the **Recent Places** section, click **Recover Unsaved Documents** and in the **Open** dialog box, select **OGC Properties((Unsaved-30122359263...** and click **Open.**

3. Save the document.

    a. On the **Recovered Unsaved File** message bar, click **Save As.** 🖫 Save As

    b. In the **Save As** dialog box, navigate to the C:\084582Data\Getting Started with Word 2010 folder.

    c. In the **File name** text box, verify that the file name is "OGC Properties.docx" and click **Save.**

4. Save a copy of the file in the Word 2003 file format.

    a. Select the **File** tab and choose **Save As.**

b. In the **Save As** dialog box, verify that the C:\084582Data\Getting Started with Word 2010 folder is selected.

c. In the **File name** text box, type *OGC Properties 97_2003* and from the **Save as type** drop-down list, select **Word 97–2003 Document (*.doc)** and click **Save.**

d. On the Quick Access toolbar, click the **Close** button to close the document.

Lesson 1 Follow-up

In this lesson, you identified and started working with basic Word 2010 tools and features to create documents. Gaining familiarity with the application and the basic set of tasks involved in creating a document not only provides the fundamental skills required to create documents with Word, but also lays the foundation to perform more complex tasks.

1. **How will the Word 2010 application add value to you at your workplace?**

2. **How will the default typing options in the Word 2010 application help you?**

2 | Editing Text in a Word Document

Lesson Time: 1 hour(s), 45 minutes

Lesson Objectives:

In this lesson, you will edit text in a Word document.

You will:

- Select text.
- Modify text.
- Find and replace text.

Introduction

You created a basic Word document and added content to it. Once you have created the basic structure of documents, you may want to perform additional editing of the text. In this lesson, you will edit Word documents.

A document goes through many changes and revisions before it is finalized. Editing a document may require you to navigate through the entire document, locate the text you want to change, and then edit it. When working on long documents, this may be a time-consuming process. To perform editing you will also need to be aware of various text selection and manipulation techniques. Word provides various tools and features which allow you to edit text with ease.

TOPIC A

Select Text

You saved a Word document and now you are ready to retrieve it and make some changes. To incorporate these changes, you need to find and select the text you want to modify. In this topic, you will navigate through a document and select the required text.

Locating and selecting text in a document are important steps in editing a document. Word documents often have multiple pages and only one page can be viewed and edited at a time. Using appropriate navigation techniques will help you locate the text you want. Word provides various interface components for navigating through a document.

Scroll Bars

In addition to using the keyboard, you can use scroll bars in Word to navigate through a document. When you navigate using scroll bars, the location of the insertion point does not change. The vertical scroll bar, located at the right of the application window, is used to scroll up or down. The horizontal scroll bar, located just above the status bar, is used to scroll to the left or right. The scroll arrows at the ends of the scroll bars allow you to scroll slowly through a document. You can drag the scroll box between the scroll bars to scroll quickly through the document.

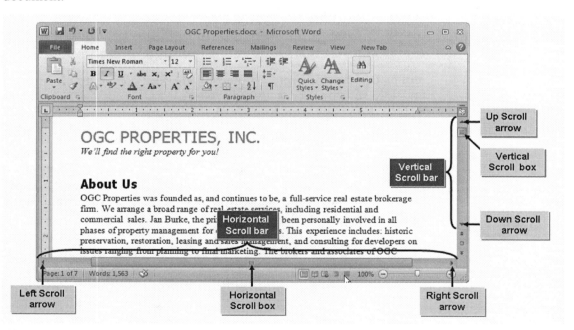

Figure 2-1: *The scroll bar components used to navigate through a document.*

The Next Page, Previous Page, and Select Browse Object Buttons

In addition to the scroll bar components, you can also use the **Next Page** and **Previous Page** buttons, located below the vertical scroll bar, to navigate through a document. By default, the **Next Page** and **Previous Page** buttons are configured to browse page-by-page. The **Select Browse Object** button, located between the **Next Page** and **Previous Page** buttons, allows you to navigate through the document by selecting an object from the object pane. Objects may include pages, sections, comments, edits, and more.

The Selection Bar

The selection bar is an area on the left margin of a document that is used to select text. When positioned on the selection bar, the mouse pointer will change from an I-beam to a right-pointing arrow. You can then click on the selection bar to select a line, double-click to select a paragraph, or triple-click to select the entire document.

How to Select Text

Procedure Reference: Navigate Through a Document and Select Text

To navigate through a document and select text:

1. Open a document.
2. Use the appropriate navigation techniques to move to the desired location.
3. Use the appropriate selection methods to select text.

Keyboard Navigation Techniques

You can use the navigation keys on the keyboard to navigate within a document.

Pressing This Key/Keys	Moves the Insertion Point
Right Arrow or **Left Arrow**	One character or space to the right or left.
Ctrl+Right Arrow or **Ctrl+Left Arrow**	One word to the right or left.
Down Arrow or **Up Arrow**	One line down or up.
Ctrl+Down Arrow or **Ctrl+Up Arrow**	One paragraph down or up.
Page Down or **Page Up**	One screen down or up.
Ctrl+Page Down or **Ctrl+ Page Up**	To the beginning of the next or previous page.
Home or **End**	To the beginning or end of a line.
Ctrl+Home or **Ctrl+End**	To the beginning or end of the document.

Scroll Bar Navigation Techniques

You can use the vertical and horizontal scroll bars to navigate to the different parts of a document without changing the position of the insertion point.

If You Need To	Do This
Scroll up or down one line at a time	On the vertical scroll bar, click the scroll up arrow or the scroll down arrow.

If You Need To	Do This
Scroll up or down multiple lines	On the vertical scroll bar, click above or below the scroll box.
Scroll to the left or right	On the horizontal scroll bar, click the scroll left arrow or the scroll right arrow, or click to the left or right of the scroll box.
Display the top, bottom, or center of a document	On the vertical scroll bar, drag the scroll box to the top, bottom, or center of the scroll bar.

Text Selection Methods

Apart from using the selection bar to select text in a document, you can select individual characters, words, sentences, paragraphs, or even the entire document by using the mouse, keyboard, or a combination of both.

To Select	Do This
Variable amounts of text	• Click and drag the mouse pointer over the text to select a block of text. • Place the insertion point at the beginning of the text, hold down **Shift,** and press an arrow key to extend the selection in the desired direction. • Place the insertion point at the beginning of the text, hold down **Shift,** and click at the end of the desired block of text.
A word	Double-click the word. This selects the trailing space after the word, but does not select punctuation after it.
A line or lines of text	Click the selection bar to the left of the line. To select multiple contiguous lines, click and drag the mouse pointer on the selection bar.
A sentence	Hold down **Ctrl** and click anywhere in the sentence. This selects the sentence and its closing punctuation.
A paragraph	Triple-click the paragraph or double-click the selection bar next to the paragraph.
Noncontiguous sections	To select items that are not adjacent, select the first item, line, or paragraph, and hold down **Ctrl** while you select additional items.
The entire document	• Triple-click the selection bar. • Press **Ctrl+A.** • On the **Home** tab, in the **Editing** group, from the **Select** drop-down list, select **Select All.**
Deselect text	Make another selection or click away from the selected text anywhere in the text area.

ACTIVITY 2-1
Selecting Text in a Word Document

Data Files:

OGC Properties.docx

Scenario:

You need to attend an important client meeting to brief them about your company. You feel that the information available in the OGC Properties.docx document will be very helpful for the client meeting. So, you decide to browse through the document, and familiarize yourself with the content.

---

1. Display different parts of the document by using the vertical scroll bar.

    a. On the Quick Access toolbar, click the **Open** button.

    b. In the **Open** dialog box, navigate to the C:\084582Data\Editing Text in a Word Document folder.

    c. Select **OGC Properties.docx** and click **Open.**

    d. On the vertical scroll bar, click the scroll bar area below the scroll box to scroll down by a screen.

    e. Click the **Next Page** button, to move the insertion point to the top of the second page of the document.

    f. On the vertical scroll bar, drag the scroll box to the bottom of the scroll bar.

---

2. Move the insertion point to different parts of the document.

    a. Drag the vertical scroll box up to navigate to the top of page 2.

    > As you drag the scroll box, you will notice a ScreenTip with the number of the current page being displayed.

    b. Click at the beginning of the paragraph that starts with the text "Relocation Package."

    c. Press the **Right Arrow** key to move the insertion point one character to the right.

    d. Press the **Left Arrow** key to move the insertion point one character to the left.

    e. Press the **Up Arrow** and **Down Arrow** keys and the **Page Up** and **Page Down** keys to move to various locations in the document.

f.   Hold down **Ctrl** and press **End** to move the insertion point to the end of the document.

3.   Select various sections of text.

a.   Hold down **Ctrl** and press **Home** to return to the beginning of the document.

b.   Place the mouse pointer to the left of the text "OGC Properties, Inc." and observe
that the mouse pointer looks like an I-beam.

c.   Click before the text "OGC Properties, Inc." and drag the mouse pointer to the end of
the text "OGC Properties, Inc." to select the entire text.

d.   Click before the text "We'll find," hold down **Shift,** and click after the paragraph mark
at the end of the text "for you!" to select the sentence.

e.   On the selection bar, move the mouse pointer to the line that begins with the text
"OGC Properties was founded" until the shape of the mouse pointer changes to a
right-pointing arrow, and then click to select that sentence.

f.   Hold down **Shift** and press the **Down Arrow** key four times to extend the selection
to include the next four lines.

g.   Triple-click the paragraph below "Description of Our Firm" to select it.

4.   Select the entire Word document.

a.   On the **Home** tab, in the **Editing** group, from the **Select** drop-down list, select **Select
All** to select all the text in the document.

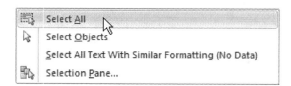

b.   Click anywhere in the text area to deselect the text.

TOPIC B
Modify Text

You selected text in a document. You will make text selections extensively when you need to make changes to text in a document. In this topic, you will modify the text in a Word document.

When you enter text, you often type words as they form in your thoughts. However, when you run through the content of the document again, chances are that you may want to add or delete some text, or even rearrange the existing text to enhance the clarity of the information in the document. Word 2010 provides options to help you achieve this task efficiently.

The Clipboard Task Pane

The *Clipboard task pane* lists the objects that are copied or cut from a document. The pane displays the content of the clipboard, a temporary storage area that stores cut or copied content. You can use this pane to display the objects that you copied from a specific location and then transfer the objects to the destination document by using the paste functionality. You can store up to 24 objects in the clipboard. When you copy items to the clipboard, the latest items will be displayed at the top of the pane. You can use the **Clipboard** task pane to paste all the clipboard objects, clear the clipboard, and to customize the task pane.

Figure 2-2: The Clipboard task pane containing items ready to be pasted.

Customization Options in the Clipboard Task Pane

The **Clipboard** task pane can be customized by using the options available in the **Options** drop-down list.

Option	Description
Show Office Clipboard Automatically	Displays the **Clipboard** task pane as soon as you open a document.

Option	Description
Show Office Clipboard When Ctrl+C Pressed Twice	Displays the **Clipboard** task pane when you press **Ctrl+C** twice.
Collect Without Showing Office Clipboard	Collects items to the clipboard without displaying the **Clipboard** task pane.
Show Office Clipboard Icon on Taskbar	Displays the Office Clipboard icon on the taskbar.
Show Status Near Taskbar When Copying	Displays a message above the Office Clipboard icon about the items that are copied to the clipboard.

Text Editing Options

Word provides you with various methods to move text or a selection of text from one location to another, within or between documents.

Method	Description
Cut and paste	After selecting text, you can move it to the clipboard and then paste it in the desired location. You can move text to the clipboard by using the options in the **Clipboard** group, the shortcut menu, or the **Ctrl+X** keyboard shortcut.
Drag	After selecting text, you can move it from the current location by directly dragging it to the desired location. When you drag text, it is not placed on the clipboard.
Copy and paste	After selecting text, you can copy it to the clipboard and then paste it in the desired location. You can copy text to the clipboard by using the options in the **Clipboard** group, the shortcut menu, or the **Ctrl+C** keyboard shortcut.

Paste Options

You can paste text or sections of text that are copied or cut, in any part of a document, by using the paste options in the **Clipboard** group.

Option	Description
Paste	Pastes the copied or cut text in the desired location.
Paste Special	Opens the **Paste Special** dialog box, where you can specify the format in which the copied or cut text should be displayed when pasted.
Set Default Paste	Displays the **Word Options** dialog box that allows you to select the default paste option.

The Paste Options Smart Tag

When you paste an item, the **Paste Options** smart tag is displayed immediately after the pasted item. The options in the smart tag enable you to specify the formatting for the pasted item.

Option	Allows You To
Keep Source Formatting	Retain the formatting that is applied to the text in the source document.
Merge Formatting	Adopt the formatting that is applied to the location where the text is pasted in the destination document.
Keep Text Only	Discard the formatting from the source text and paste just plain text.
Use Destination Theme	Copy the content in the source document without the formatting.

Live Preview

Live Preview is a feature that enables users to preview the results of applying design and formatting changes to a document, without actually applying them. These changes are displayed in the document as soon as the user moves the mouse pointer over the available options in a gallery.

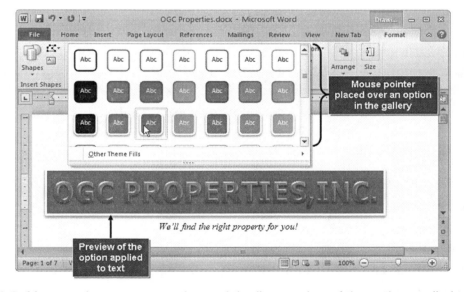

Figure 2-3: *Mouse pointer over an option and the live preview of the option applied to the text.*

Paste Preview Options

In Word 2010, you can use the paste preview functionality, which is an integration of the Live Preview feature with the paste functionality, to preview the changes before pasting them.

The Undo Command

The Undo command helps you correct unnecessary or erroneous actions. You can undo an action by clicking the **Undo** button on the Quick Access toolbar or by pressing **Ctrl+Z.** By clicking the drop-down arrow next to the **Undo** button, you can view the actions that were performed earlier, listed in reverse order. Deleted items, which are not collected by the **Clipboard** task pane, can be restored only by using the **Undo** command.

The Redo Command

The **Redo** button on the Quick Access toolbar allows you to redo a series of actions in the reverse order in which the changes were undone. The Redo command works only for the current working session. Once you close a document, the Redo list is cleared.

 While you can undo or redo most actions, certain actions that involve accessing files, such as opening, saving, or printing a document, cannot be undone. Only the actions that have been undone can be redone.

How to Modify Text

Procedure Reference: Insert or Delete Text

To insert or delete text:

1. Place the insertion point where you want to insert new text, or select text that you want to overwrite.
2. Type text that you want to insert.
3. If necessary, delete text.
   - Place the insertion point at the desired location and press **Backspace** to delete characters to the left of the insertion point.
   - Place the insertion point at the desired location and press **Delete** to delete characters to the right of the insertion point.
   - Select a block of text and press **Delete** to delete a block of text.

Procedure Reference: Move or Copy Text

To move or copy text to a new location:

1. Select the text that you want to move or copy.
2. Cut or copy the selected text.
   - On the **Home** tab, in the **Clipboard** group, click the **Cut** or **Copy** button or;
   - Press **Ctrl+X** to cut or press **Ctrl+C** to copy or;
   - Right-click the selected text and choose **Cut** or **Copy.**
3. Place the insertion point at the location where you want to move or copy the text.
4. Paste text.
   - On the **Home** tab, in the **Clipboard** group, click the **Paste** drop-down arrow, and in the displayed gallery, select a paste option.
   - Paste text with default paste settings.
     - On the **Home** tab, in the **Clipboard** group, click the **Paste** button or;

- Press **Ctrl+V** or;
- Right-click and choose **Paste.**
- Paste text using the **Clipboard.**
    a. On the **Home** tab, in the **Clipboard** group, click the **Clipboard** dialog box launcher.
    b. In the **Clipboard** task pane, in the **Click an item to paste** list box, select a copied item to paste it.
    c. If necessary, in the **Clipboard** task pane, click **Paste All** to paste all the items in the clipboard in the document.
    d. If necessary, click **Clear All** to clear the clipboard.

5. To move or copy multiple text selections, cut or copy each selection to the clipboard.
6. Open the **Clipboard** task pane and make the appropriate choice to paste in multiple selections.
    - In the **Click an item to paste** list box, select items one after the other to paste them in the specified location.
    - Click **Paste All** to paste all the items in the clipboard in the specified location.

Procedure Reference: Undo or Redo Actions

To undo or redo actions:

1. Undo an action.
    - On the Quick Access toolbar, click the **Undo** button.
    - Press **Ctrl+Z.**
    - Click the **Undo** drop-down arrow to display a list of actions and select an action to undo all the action up to the selected action.
2. If necessary, redo an action.
    - Click the **Redo** button or;
    - Press **Ctrl+Y.**
3. If necessary undo or redo more actions.

ACTIVITY 2-2
Modifying Text

Data Files:

Nolan Letter.docx

Before You Begin:

The OGC Properties.docx file is open.

Scenario:

While reviewing the draft document of OGC Properties, you notice that some of the text is out of place. On page one, you feel that the "Our Company Affiliations" heading and the paragraph that immediately follows it should be moved down the document so that they precede the paragraph on page two, which begins with "Buying a Home." You also realize that some content is missing from the draft document, specifically, a list of things a realtor does for clients under the "Selling Your Home" paragraph on page two, and the OGC Properties guarantee on page three, below the "Our Guarantee" paragraph. Fortunately, you recall seeing that information in a letter written to Beth Nolan.

You are told that the Kentucky, Ohio, and Texas offices of the company you are working for, will be closed soon. You need to delete those items from the OGC Properties Locations list. Before you complete editing the document, you find out that what you heard about the offices being closed was a miscommunication. You will need to restore those three blocks of text to the list of offices.

---

1. Delete an unnecessary word from the OGC Properties document.

    a. In the OGC Properties document, under the title "Description of Our Firm," in the first line, click before the word "The."

    b. Press **Delete** four times to delete the word and the trailing space after it.

---

2. Insert text in the "About Us" paragraph.

    a. Under the title "About Us," in the second sentence that begins with "We arrange," click before the word "services" to place the insertion point.

    b. Type *real estate* and press the **Spacebar.**

---

3. Move the "Our Company Affiliations" paragraph to the second page.

    a. In the document, click before the title "Our Company Affiliations."

    b. Drag the vertical scroll box down till the bottom of the scroll box is in line with the "About us" title, to view the paragraph below the title "Our Company Affiliations."

    c. Hold down **Shift,** and click the blank line below the "Our Company Affiliations" paragraph.

    d. On the **Home** tab, in the **Clipboard** group, click the **Cut** button.

---

e. Press **Page Down** twice to navigate to the middle of the next page.

f. Place the insertion point at the beginning of the "Buying a Home" heading.

g. On the **Home** tab, in the **Clipboard** group, click the **Paste** drop-down arrow.

h. In the displayed gallery, in the **Paste Options** section, place the mouse pointer over **Merge Formatting**, which is the second option, and observe a preview of the text pasted in the document.

i. Select the **Merge Formatting** option to paste the text along with the formatting of the location.

j. On the **Home** tab, in the **Clipboard** group, click the **Clipboard** dialog box launcher to display the **Clipboard** task pane.

4. Copy the necessary text from the Nolan Letter.docx file.

a. Navigate to the C:\084582Data\Editing Text in a Word Document folder and open the Nolan Letter.docx file.

b. In the Nolan Letter file, click before the text "Here's what a realtor does for you," hold down **Shift,** and click after the paragraph marker after the text "buyer."

c. On the **Home** tab, in the **Clipboard** group, click the **Copy** button to copy the selection to the **Clipboard.**

d. Press **Page Down** to reach the end of the document.

e. In the last paragraph, select the entire sentence that begins with the text "We are so sure."

f. Hold down **Ctrl** and press **C** to copy the selection and add it to the clipboard.

5. Use the **Clipboard** task pane to paste copied text.

a. Select the **View** tab, and in the **Window** group, from the **Switch Windows** drop-down list, select **2 OGC Properties** to switch to the OGC Properties window.

b. Scroll up to display the lower half of page 1.

c. In the blank line above the text "Relocation Package" click to place the insertion point.

d. In the **Clipboard** task pane, in the **Click an item to paste** list box, observe the items in the clipboard and select the item that begins with the text "Here's what a realtor" to paste it in the document.

e. Hold down **Ctrl** and press **Page Down** to navigate to the next page.

f. Below the text "Our Guarantee," in the blank line, place the insertion point.

g. In the **Clipboard** task pane, in the **Click an item to paste** list box, select the item that begins with the text "We are so sure" to paste it in the document.

h. In the **Clipboard** task pane, click **Clear All** to clear all the items that were copied to the clipboard.

i. At the top-right corner of the **Clipboard** task pane, click the **Close** button to close the task pane. ✖

6. Delete the unnecessary text.

a. Scroll down to display all the locations in page 3.

b. Select "Kentucky," "Lexington," and the blank line following "Lexington."

c. Press **Delete** to delete the selection.

d. Select "Ohio," "Cleveland," "Toledo," and the blank line following "Toledo," and delete them.

e. Delete "Texas," "Dallas," and "San Antonio."

7. Undo the deletions.

a. On the Quick Access toolbar, click the **Undo** button, to restore the text "Texas, Dallas," and "San Antonio." ↩▾

b. Click the **Undo** button twice to restore both the "Ohio" and "Kentucky" text blocks.

8. Save the document.

a. Select the **View** tab, and in the **Window** group, from the **Switch Windows** drop-down list, select **1 Nolan Letter** to switch to the Nolan Letter window.

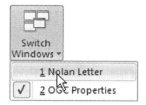

b. On the Quick Access toolbar, click the **Close** button to close the Nolan Letter.docx document.

c. Select the **File** tab and choose **Save as.**

d. In the **Save As** dialog box, in the **File name** text box, type *My OGC Properties* and click **Save.**

TOPIC C
Find and Replace Text

You modified text in a Word document. When modifying text in a document, you may sometimes need to search for and replace a specific word or phrase in the document. In this topic, you will find and replace text in a Word document.

If you are manually searching for a piece of text in a large document, it can be like looking for a needle in a haystack. If you need to search for and replace all occurrences of the text, it will not only take a very long time to search for the text, but you may also end up missing a few occurrences. Word provides a simple and efficient way to search for and replace text in a document, without spending hours on it.

The Navigation Pane

The *Navigation pane* provides multiple options to navigate through and search for information in a document. The **Browse the results from your current search** tab in this pane allows you to enter text that is to be searched for in the entire document. It then lists all the instances of the search text found in the document and enables you to navigate to any instance in the document by clicking on it in the pane. All instances of the searched text are also highlighted in the document. The **Navigation** pane also contains options to search for graphics, tables, and equations in the document.

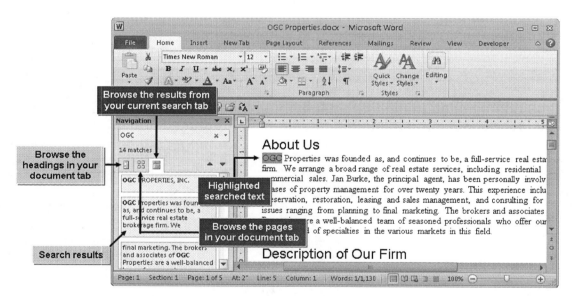

Figure 2-4: The Navigation pane highlighting the occurrence of the word being searched for.

Additional Functions of the Navigation Pane

In addition to using the **Navigation** pane to perform search and replace operations, you can also navigate a lengthy document using the other tabs in the pane. The **Browse the headings in your document** tab allows you to navigate through a document if the document has content with heading styles applied. You can also delete sections of text within headings and move sections of text up or down a document. The **Browse the pages in your document** tab provides options to browse through a document based on a thumbnail view of the pages.

The Find and Replace Dialog Box

The **Find and Replace** dialog box contains three tabs that assist you in finding and replacing text in a Word document.

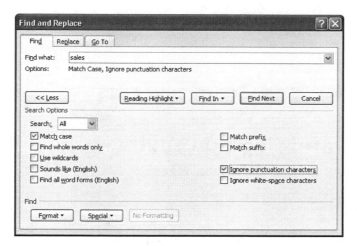

Figure 2-5: The Find and Replace dialog box displaying options on the Find tab.

Tab	Description
Find	Provides various **Find** options that help you specify the search criteria.
Replace	Provides options to replace found text with desired text. The keyboard shortcut, **Ctrl+H,** displays the **Find and Replace** dialog box with the **Replace** tab selected.
Go To	Provides options that let you specify the exact location in the document where you want to navigate to. The keyboard shortcut, **Ctrl+G,** displays the **Find and Replace** dialog box with the **Go To** tab selected.

Finding and Replacing Text by Using the Select Browse Object Button

The Select Browse Object button contains the Find icon and the Go To icon which can be used to open the **Find and Replace** dialog box with the **Find** tab and **Go To** tab selected respectively.

The Find Options Dialog Box

The **Find Options** dialog box allows you to modify the default behavior of the Find feature in Word according to your search requirements. It contains an assortment of options to search a Word document with specific search criteria. The **Find Options** dialog box can be accessed by selecting **Options** from the **Find Options and additional search commands** drop-down list in the **Navigation** pane.

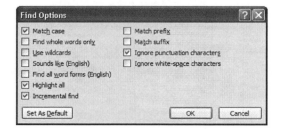

Figure 2-6: Search options set in the Find Options dialog box.

How to Find and Replace Text

Procedure Reference: Find and Replace Text

To find and replace text in a document:

1. Open a document.
2. On the **Home** tab, in the **Editing** group, click **Replace.**
3. In the **Find and Replace** dialog box, select the **Find** tab, and in the **Find what** text box, type the text that you want to locate. You can also use wildcard characters to expand the search.
4. If necessary, on the **Find** tab, specify the desired settings.
    *   Click the **More** button and set the advanced search options.

 Advanced search options include specifying whether to search up or down a page; match casing; find whole words or sections of words; and include punctuation, white spaces, and formatting in search criteria.

*   From the **Reading Highlight** drop-down list, select **Highlight All** to highlight all the instances of the search criteria in the document.
*   Click **Find In** to locate every occurrence of the text in the document.
*   Click **Find Next** to locate the next occurrence of the text in the document. Continue clicking **Find Next** to advance to the next occurrences.
5. In the **Find and Replace** dialog box, select the **Replace** tab.
6. In the **Replace with** text box, type the text that you want to substitute for the found occurrences. Include any special characters such as tabs or double spaces.

 To directly display the **Replace** tab in the **Find and Replace** dialog box, either click **Replace** in the **Editing** group or press **Ctrl+H.**

7. If necessary, on the **Replace** tab, search for and replace text.
    *   Click **Replace** to replace the highlighted text and continue searching for the next occurrence.
    *   Click **Replace All** to replace all occurrences of the text simultaneously.
    *   Click **Find Next** to find the next occurrence of the word.

If you change your mind about a replace operation, click the **Undo** button on the Quick Access toolbar. If you used the **Replace** button, Word will undo the replacements one by one. If you used the **Replace All** button, Word will undo all the replacements at the same time.

8. In the **Microsoft Word** message box, click **OK** to complete the search and replace operation.

9. In the **Find and Replace** dialog box, click **Close.**

Character Formatting and Special Character

The **Format** button in the **Find and Replace** dialog box allows access to options which enable you to find text with specific formatting, such as font color and font style, and replace or remove the formatting. The **Special** button provides access to options which enable you to find and replace special characters, such as paragraph marks, and tab characters.

Procedure Reference: Search for Components Using the Go To Command

To search for components using the **Go To** command:

1. Display the **Go To** tab in the **Find and Replace** dialog box.

   - On the **Home** tab, in the **Editing** group, from the **Find** drop-down list, select **Go To** or;

   - In the **Navigation** pane, from the **Find Options and additional search commands** drop-down list, select **Go To.**

   - Press **Ctrl+G** or;

   - On the status bar, click the **Page Number** button or;

   - On the vertical scroll bar, click the **Select Browse Object** button and from the displayed options, select **Go To.**

2. In the **Find and Replace** dialog box, on the **Go To** tab, in the **Go to what** list box, select the component that you want to go to, such as a page, section, or line.

3. In the **Enter <component>** text box, enter a value and click **Go To.**

4. Click **Close** to close the **Find and Replace** dialog box.

ACTIVITY 2-3
Finding and Replacing Text

Before You Begin:

The My OGC Properties.docx file is open.

Scenario:

When preparing the OGC Properties document, "OGC Properties" was not properly capitalized in all the instances. Both "OGC" and the "P" in "Properties" should always be capitalized. Moreover, as part of a new Human Resources department initiative, many job titles have been updated. You want to make sure that the job title "broker" is changed to "agent." You also notice that a heading on page two needs to be modified.

1. Search the document for instances of the text "ogc properties" and highlight them.

   a. Scroll up and place the insertion point at the beginning of the document.

   b. Select the **Home** tab, and in the **Editing** group, click **Replace**.

   c. In the **Find and Replace** dialog box, select the **Find** tab and then click **More** to display the **Search Options** section.

   d. In the **Search Options** section, check the **Match case** check box.

   e. Click **Less** to hide the advanced options in the **Find and Replace** dialog box.

   f. In the **Find what** text box, click and type *ogc properties* in lower case.

   g. From the **Reading Highlight** drop-down list, select **Highlight All** to highlight all instances of the text.

   h. Scroll through the document and observe that all instances of the found text are highlighted.

2. Change the casing of the text "ogc properties" in all the instances.

   a. In the **Find and Replace** dialog box, select the **Replace** tab to display the replace options.

b.   Click in the **Replace with** text box and type *OGC Properties* in the given casing.

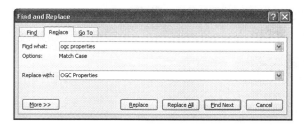

c.   Click **Find Next** to find the first occurrence of the text, "ogc properties."

d.   Click **Replace** to replace the wrong instance with the right one.

e.   Click **Replace All** to replace the text in all instances.

f.   When Word finishes searching the document and completes all replacements, in the **Microsoft Word** message box, click **OK.**

3.   Set new search and replace criteria.

a.   In the **Find and Replace** dialog box, in the **Find what** text box, type *broker*

b.   Press **Tab** to move the insertion point to the **Replace with** text box.

c.   Type *agent*

d.   Click **More** to display the advanced search options.

e.   Uncheck the **Match case** check box.

f.   Click **Less** to hide the advanced options in the **Find and Replace** dialog box.

4.   Find and replace the appropriate instances of the word "broker" with "agent."

a.   In the My OGC Properties – Microsoft Word window, click the document, hold down **Ctrl** and press **Home** to move the insertion point to the beginning of the document.

b.   Click **Find Next** to find the first occurrence of the word "broker."

c.   In the first occurrence, observe that "broker" is part of the word "brokerage." Click **Find Next** to ignore that occurrence and to continue the search.

d.   In the next occurrence, click **Replace** to replace "broker" with "agent" and continue the search.

e.   Click **Replace** to continue searching and replacing appropriate occurrences of the word "broker" with "agent."

f.   When you have finished, in the **Microsoft Word** message box, click **OK** to end the search and replace operation.

5.   Navigate to the second page to delete the unnecessary text.

a.   In the **Find and Replace** dialog box, select the **Go To** tab.

b.   In the **Go to what** list box, verify that **Page** is selected.

c.   In the **Enter page number** text box, type *2*

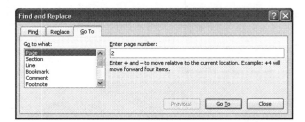

d.   Click **Go To** to place the insertion point at the beginning of the second page.

e.   In the **Find and Replace** dialog box, click **Close** to close the dialog box.

f.   In the heading "Special Network," double-click the word "Special" to select it along with the space after it.

g.   Press **Delete** to delete the selected text.

h.   Save and close the document.

Lesson 2 Follow-up

In this lesson, you edited a document by using a number of editing techniques such as moving and copying text, undoing changes, and replacing text. These basic editing skills will form the foundation of all the tasks that you will perform on Microsoft Word documents.

1. **What Word components will you use most often when editing a Word document?**

2. **How will the editing techniques in Word help you work more efficiently?**

3 Modifying the Appearance of Text in a Word Document

Lesson Time: 1 hour(s), 45 minutes

Lesson Objectives:

In this lesson, you will modify the appearance of text in a Word document.

You will:

- Apply character formatting.
- Align text using tabs.
- Display text as list items.
- Modify the layout of a paragraph.
- Apply styles.
- Manage formatting.
- Apply borders and shading.

Introduction

You edited text in a Word document. The next step is to change the formatting of text to make it visually appealing. In this lesson, you will modify the appearance of text by using various formatting options in Word 2010.

Imagine you have two documents that are completely identical, except for the fact that one incorporates formatting to distinguish document elements and the other does not. The document that has appropriate formatting applied to it is easier to read than the one with just the default text style. By properly formatting text in Word documents, you can enhance their readability and visual appeal.

TOPIC A
Apply Character Formatting

You searched for and replaced text in a Word document. In addition to ensuring the accuracy of text in a document, you may want to modify the appearance of text by changing the font style. In this topic, you will apply character formatting in a Word document.

While reading a newspaper or a magazine, your eyes automatically dart toward text that is presented in different styles or varying sizes, or with other effects. These enhancements can focus readers on the important information. Choosing the appropriate text formatting for your documents can provide visual cues to help your readers understand the content.

Fonts

Definition:

A *font* is a predefined typeface with a unique design and character spacing. You can specify different styles and sizes for the fonts in a document. The set of characters in a font includes letters, numbers, and punctuation marks. A document can have more than one font applied to the text it contains. You can modify the basic appearance of a font by using various font formatting options.

Example:

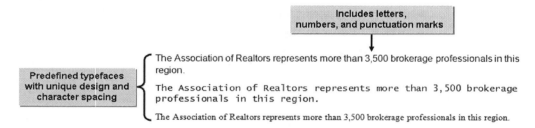

Figure 3-1: *Different types of fonts applied to a text.*

The Mini Toolbar

The **Mini Toolbar** is a floating toolbar that appears when you select text in a document. It is displayed above the selected text and includes options to format text, without having to move to the Ribbon. This toolbar disappears when you move the mouse pointer away from the selection. You can also invoke the Mini toolbar, along with a list of other commands, by right-clicking anywhere in the document.

Figure 3-2: *The Mini Toolbar displaying the various font formatting options.*

Font Options

Word provides you with various options to change the appearance of fonts. You can change the font size, color, emphasis properties, case, and effects. You can apply these options from the Mini toolbar, by using the options in the **Font** group on the **Home** tab, or in the **Font** dialog box.

Option	Description
Grow Font	Increases the font size by one point each time you click it.
Shrink Font	Decreases the font size by one point each time you click it.
Subscript	Decreases the font size and moves the text below the text baseline.
Superscript	Decreases the font size and moves the text above the text line.
Bold	Bold formats the selected text.
Italic	Italicizes the selected text.
Underline	Provides different underlining format.

Option	Description
Sentence case	Capitalizes the first letter of every sentence in the selected text.
lowercase	Converts all the characters of the selected text into small letters.
UPPERCASE	Capitalizes all the characters of the selected text.
Capitalize Each Word	Capitalizes the first letter of each word in the selected text.
tOGGLE cASE	Inverts the current capitalization of the selection. Lowercase letters become uppercase, and vice versa.
Strikethrough	Runs a line through the selected text. This effect is conventionally used to denote information that was deleted.
Double strikethrough	Runs two lines through the selected text. This effect is used when more emphasis is needed than what is provided by a single strikethrough.
Small caps	Converts all the characters in the selected text to uppercase, but reduces them to dimensions similar to lowercase characters. However, any capital letters converted to small caps will be slightly larger than the rest of the letters.
All caps	Capitalizes all the characters of the selected text, resulting in all the characters being the same size.
Hidden	Hides the selected text.

Text Highlighting Options

Highlighting text draws attention to important information in a document. The default text highlight color in a Word document is yellow. You can turn on the highlighter by clicking the **Text Highlight Color** button in the **Font** group. The mouse pointer changes to an I-beam with a highlighter when you place it over a block of text. You can then select the text to apply the default yellow highlight. You can also modify the text highlight color by selecting a color from the **Text Highlight Color** drop-down list. The selected color will be displayed on the **Text Highlight Color** button. The highlighter remains active until you turn it off by clicking the **Text Highlight Color** button again.

Highlighter Printing Tip

If you are going to print a document by using a black and white printer, use a light color or gray to highlight text. This ensures that the text will still be readable.

The Format Painter

The *Format Painter* is a formatting tool that allows you to copy the character or paragraph formatting in the selected text and apply it to one or more additional selections. It can also be used to apply some basic graphics formatting. The **Format Painter** does not provide any formatting option of its own.

How to Apply Character Formatting

Procedure Reference: Change a Font Style

To change a font style:

1.   Select the text you want to change.

2.   Apply a different font.

- On the **Home** tab, in the **Font** group, from the **Font** drop-down list, select the desired font or;

- On the **Home** tab, in the **Font** group, click the **Font** dialog box launcher, and in the **Font** dialog box, in the **Font** list box, select a font and click **OK** or;

- On the Mini toolbar, from the **Font** drop-down list, select the desired font.

3.   Set the font color.

- On the **Home** tab, in the **Font** group, from the **Font Color** drop-down list, select a color or;

- On the Mini toolbar, from the **Font Color** drop-down list, select a color or;

- In the **Font** dialog box, from the **Font color** drop-down list, select a color and click **OK.**

4. Set the desired font size.

- On the **Home** tab, in the **Font** group, from the **Font Size** drop-down list, select the desired font size or;
- On the **Home** tab, in the **Font** group, click the **Grow Font** or **Shrink Font** button to increase or decrease the font size by one point at a time or;
- Open the **Font** dialog box and select the desired font size in the **Size** list box or;
- On the Mini toolbar, from the **Font Size** drop-down list, select the desired font size or;
- On the Mini toolbar, click the **Grow Font** or **Shrink Font** button to increase or decrease the font size by one point at a time.

5. Apply the required font styles.

- On the **Home** tab, in the **Font** group, click any combination of the **Bold, Italic,** and **Underline** buttons to bold format, italicize, or underline the selected text or;
- In the **Font** dialog box, in the **Font style** list box, select **Regular, Italic, Bold,** or **Bold Italic,** and then select an underline style from the **Underline style** drop-down list or;
- On the Mini toolbar, click any combination of the **Regular, Italic,** and **Bold** buttons to apply the styles for the fonts.

6. Apply the required font effects.

- On the **Home** tab, in the **Font** group, select the desired font effect or;
- In the **Font** dialog box, in the **Effects** section, check the desired check boxes to apply the desired font effects.

7. On the **Home** tab, in the **Font** group, from the **Change Case** drop-down list, select the desired font case.

8. Apply a highlight color.

- On the **Home** tab, in the **Font** group, click the **Text Highlight Color** button to apply the default color or;
- On the **Home** tab, in the **Font** group, click the **Text Highlight Color** drop-down arrow and select a color from the displayed gallery or;
- On the Mini toolbar, click the **Text Highlight Color** drop-down arrow, and from the displayed gallery, select a highlight color.

Procedure Reference: Copy Formatting Using the Format Painter

To copy formatting using the Format Painter:

1. Select the text that has the formatting you want to duplicate.

2. On the **Home** tab, in the **Clipboard** group, click the **Format Painter** button.

3. Select the text to which you want to copy the formatting.

 If you double-click the **Format Painter** button, it will remain active, and you can make additional selections to continue copying the formatting.

4. If necessary, click the **Format Painter** button again or press **Esc** to deactivate the Format Painter.

Repeat an Action vs. Redo an Action

After you perform an action such as formatting text, you can quickly repeat the action by clicking the **Repeat** button on the Quick Access toolbar. To see what action is going to be repeated, point to the **Repeat** button; the name of the last action you performed will be appended to the **Repeat** button's ScreenTip. You can also repeat actions by pressing **F4** or **Ctrl+Y.**

Repeat is not the same as **Redo.** You can repeat any action, but the **Redo** command works only if you have first used the **Undo** command to undo a specific action.

ACTIVITY 3-1
Changing the Appearance of a Font

Data Files:

C:\084582Data\Modifying the Appearance of Text in a Word Document\OGC Properties.docx

Scenario:

You have created a company report that will be sent to all the clients. However, while review-ing the document, you realize that some critical information might be lost amidst the pages of plain text. You need to ensure that the clients do not miss this critical information, even if they only glance through the document. So, you decide to apply formatting to the critical text.

---

1. Format the company name at the beginning of the document.

   a. From the C:\084582Data\Modifying the Appearance of Text in a Word Document folder, open the OGC Properties.docx file.

   b. Select the heading "OGC Properties,Inc."

   c. On the **Home** tab, in the **Font** group, from the **Font** drop-down list, in the **All Fonts** section, select **Arial.**

   d. From the **Font Size** drop-down list, select **22.**

   e. From the **Change Case** drop-down list, select **UPPERCASE** to convert all the letters in the title to upper case.

   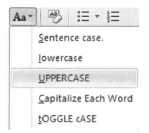

    f.   Click the **Font Color** drop-down arrow, and in the displayed gallery, in the **Standard Colors** section, select **Light Blue,** which is the seventh color from the left.

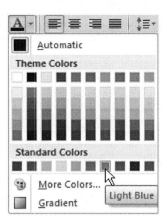

    g.   Observe that the text is now displayed in blue and click at the beginning of the next line to deselect the text.

2.   Italicize the text "We'll find the right property for you!"

    a.   Below the title, select the text "We'll find the right property for you!"

    b.   On the **Home** tab, in the **Font** group, click the **Italic** button.

3.   Repeat the italic font style on the text "unconditionally guarantee."

    a.   Scroll down to the bottom of the third page.

    b.   Under the title "Our Guarantee" in the second line, select the text "unconditionally guarantee."

    c.   On the Quick Access toolbar, click the **Repeat Italic** button, which is the fourth button from the left.

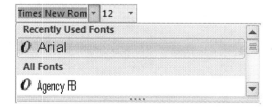

4.   Change the font of the text "Our Relocation Services."

    a.   Scroll up to the second page to display the title "Our Relocation Services," and select the title "Our Relocation Services."

    b.   On the **Home** tab, in the **Font** group, from the **Font** drop-down list, in the **Recently Used Fonts** section, select **Arial.**

c.   From the **Font Size** drop-down list, select **18.**

5.   Apply the same formatting to other titles.

    a.   On the **Home** tab, in the **Clipboard** group, click the **Format Painter** button.

    b.   Observe that the mouse pointer changes to an I-beam with a paint brush.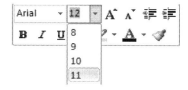

    c.   Scroll down to the bottom of the first page to display both the titles "Our Relocation Staff" and "Our Relocation Fees."

    d.   Click and drag over the title "Our Relocation Staff."

    e.   On the **Home** tab, in the **Clipboard** group, click the **Format Painter** button.

    f.   Click and drag over the title "Our Relocation Fees."

6.   Format the inline title, "Relocation Network."

    a.   If necessary scroll up to view the inline title "Relocation Network."

    b.   Select the inline title "Relocation Network."

    c.   Move the mouse pointer over the Mini toolbar until it is clearly visible.

    d.   On the Mini toolbar, from the **Font** drop-down list, select **Arial.**

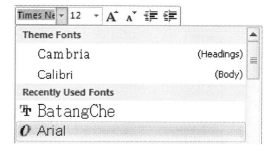

    e.   From the **Font Size** drop-down list, select **11.**

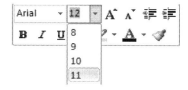

7.   Apply the double underline effect.

    a.   On the **Home** tab, in the **Font** group, click the **Font** dialog box launcher.

b. Observe that the font settings displayed in the **Font** dialog box match those of the selected text. From the **Underline Style** drop-down list, select the double underline option, and click **OK** to apply the formatting.

8. Copy the formatting of the text "Relocation Network" and apply it to the remaining five inline titles.

a. On the **Home** tab, in the **Clipboard** group, double click the **Format Painter** button to copy the formatting of the selected text.

b. Click and drag the mouse pointer over the inline title "Relocation package" to apply the copied text formatting.

c. Click and drag the mouse pointer over the inline title "Relocation Team" to apply the copied text formatting.

d. Similarly, in the successive paragraphs, apply the same formatting to "Sales Associates," "Corporate Division," and "Network."

e. On the **Home** tab, in the **Clipboard** group, click the **Format Painter** button to deselect it.

f. Save the document as *My OGC Properties* in the DOCX format.

ACTIVITY 3-2
Highlighting Text in a Document

Before You Begin:

The My OGC Properties.docx file is open.

Scenario:

You want your manager to review the fee percentages in the company report that you have created. You need to ensure that the fee percentage information stands out from the remaining text in the document. You also want to lay extra emphasis on the money back feature offered by your company.

---

1. Highlight the text "money back" in yellow.

   a. Scroll down to the end of the third page and below the title "Our Guarantee," select the text "money back."

   b. On the **Home** tab, in the **Font** group, click the **Text Highlight Color** drop-down arrow, and from the displayed gallery, select **Yellow.**

---

2. Highlight the text "5%–10%" in red.

   a. Scroll up to the bottom of the second page, and in the paragraph under the title "Our Relocation Fees," select the text "5%–10%."

b. On the **Home** tab, in the **Font** group, click the **Text Highlight Color** drop-down arrow, and from the displayed gallery, select **Red** to highlight the text in red and save the document.

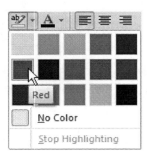

TOPIC B
Align Text Using Tabs

You applied character formatting to text in a Word document. In addition to formatting the appearance of characters, you will often have to align and space text in a document to improve readability. In this topic, you will align paragraphs in a Word document by using tab stops.

A paragraph that is not properly aligned with the margin will look poorly structured and less readable. By altering the spacing between text, you can optimally distribute the flow of text between margins. This gives text a neat appearance and enhances the information flow on a page. You can use tab stops in Word to ensure that information in a document is presented neatly and is easy to read.

Tabs

Definition:

Tabs or *tab stops* are document formatting options that enable you to align text to a specific horizontal location. You can set one or more tab stops within a paragraph of text. When you press **Tab,** the next piece of text that you type or that is already typed on that line will align with the next tab stop within the paragraph. You can use tabs to align text to the left, right, or center of the tab stop, or you can set other specialized tab types. By default, Word sets a left tab stop every half inch, within every paragraph.

Example:

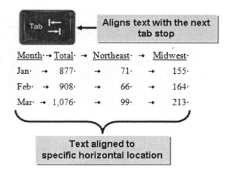

Figure 3-3: Text aligned using Tabs.

Rulers

Word provides you with measuring tools, called *rulers,* to assist you in aligning elements within a document. Rulers help you identify and change the tab settings and other document layout options such as page margins. By default, the unit of measurement for rulers is inches. However, you can change this to centimeters, millimeters, points, or picas, depending on your requirements. There are two rulers in Word—the horizontal ruler that is displayed at the top of a document and the vertical ruler that is displayed at the extreme left. By default, the rulers are turned off. You can use the **Show** group on the **View** tab or the **View Ruler** button above the vertical scroll bar to display or hide the rulers.

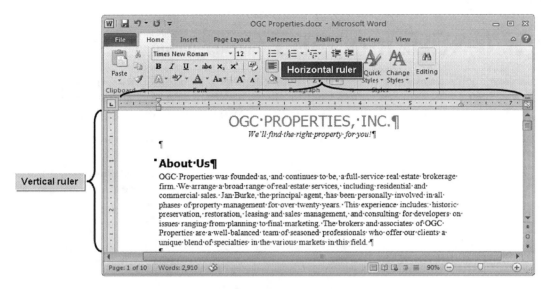

Figure 3-4: *The two rulers available in Word.*

Tab Stops on a Ruler

You can use the tab selector above the vertical ruler to set five types of tab stops.

Tab	Description
The **Left Tab** stop ⌊L⌋	Sets the left edge of the text at the tab position and allows the text to flow to the right of the tab stop.
The **Center Tab** stop ⊥	Centers the text around the tab position.
The **Right Tab** stop ⌐	Sets the right edge of the text at the tab position and allows the text to flow to the left of the tab stop.
The **Decimal Tab** stop ⊥	Aligns the decimal point of numbers to the tab position, when numbers are used.
The **Bar Tab** stop ‖	Adds a vertical line through the paragraph, at the tab position.

 To display accurate measurements correct to 0.01 of an inch in the ruler, hold down **Alt** as you drag the tabs.

The Tabs Dialog Box

You can set and clear tab stops by using the options in the **Tabs** dialog box.

Figure 3-5: The Tabs dialog box displaying the various tab setting options.

Option	Allows You To
Tab stop position	Specify the location of the tab stop on the ruler.
Default tab stops	Specify the spacing between the default tab stops.
Alignment	Change the alignment of tab stops.
Leader	Add leader characters, such as dots, dashes, or lines, that fill the space before a tab stop.
Set	Set a tab stop at the position specified in the **Tab stop position** text box.
Clear	Clear a tab stop at the position specified in the **Tab stop position** text box.
Clear All	Clear all the tab stops on the ruler.

How to Align Text Using Tabs

Procedure Reference: Set or Remove Tabs

To set or remove tabs:

1. Select the paragraph or paragraphs for which you need to set tab stops.
2. Display the rulers.
   - Above the vertical scroll bar, click the **View Ruler** button or;
   - Select the **View** tab, and in the **Show** group, check the **Rulers** check box.
3. Select the tab type.
   - Click the tab selector until the desired tab is displayed or;
   - Set the tab type in the **Paragraph** dialog box.
     a. On the **Home** tab, in the **Paragraph** group, click the **Paragraph** dialog box launcher to display the **Paragraph** dialog box.
     b. In the **Paragraph** dialog box, click the **Tabs** button to open the **Tabs** dialog box.
     c. In the **Tabs** dialog box, in the **Alignment** section, select a tab type and click **OK.**
4. Select the position to place the tab stops.
   - On the horizontal ruler, at the desired point, click to set the tab stop. To set more tabs of the same type, click additional locations or;
   - In the **Tabs** dialog box, in the **Tab stop position** text box, type the desired position for each tab and click **Set.** When you finish setting all the tabs, click **OK.**
5. Display the **Tabs** dialog box and set the tab options.
   - In the **Alignment** section, select a tab type to change the alignment of an existing tab.
   - In the **Leader** section, select the desired leader character.
6. If necessary, move the tab stop.
   - Drag a tab stop to a new position on the horizontal ruler or;
   - Change the position of the tab stops by using the **Tabs** dialog box.
     a. In the **Paragraph** dialog box, click the **Tabs** button to open the **Tabs** dialog box.
     b. In the **Alignment** section, select the desired tab stop.
     c. In the **Tab stop position** text box, specify the position to which you want the tab stop to be moved.
7. If necessary, in the **Tabs** dialog box, in the **Tab stop position** list, select a tab stop and click **Clear** to clear a tab stop or click **Clear All** to clear all the tabs for a paragraph.

ACTIVITY 3-3
Setting Tab Stops to Align Text

Before You Begin:
The My OGC Properties.docx file is open.

Scenario:
You have to send the document containing the sales data to all the regional managers in the company. Before sending it, you want to make sure that the sales data is structured properly and is formatted to ensure readability.

1. Select the sales data.

   a. Scroll up to the top of the second page.

   b. Above the vertical scroll bar, click the **View Ruler** button to display the horizontal and vertical rulers.

   c. Below the text "First-Quarter Data," click before the word "Month."

   d. Hold down **Shift** and click after "96" to select the sales data.

2. Set the right tab stops on the horizontal ruler.

   a. Above the vertical ruler, click the tab selector twice to display the **Right Tab** stop.

   b. On the horizontal ruler, click at the 1-inch mark to insert a right tab stop.

   c. Similarly, insert right tab stops at 2, 3, 4, 5, and 6 inches.

3. Align the text to the tabs.

   a. In the sales data, click before the word "Total" and press **Tab.**

   b. Click before the word "Northeast" and press **Tab.**

   c. Similarly, insert tabs before the words "Midwest," "South," "West," and "% Sold."

    d.   In the line displaying data for January insert tabs before the numbers 877, 71, 155, 406, 247, and 85.

    e.   Similarily, align the data for February and March.

    f.   Save the document.

TOPIC C

Display Text as List Items

You used tab stops to align text and improve the readability of a document. While reviewing the document, you may come across content that can be better presented if displayed in a sequential order. In this topic, you will display text as list items.

Using lists can greatly improve the clarity and readability of text by breaking the information into appropriate chunks. Procedural information or instructions presented in the form of a list is easier to follow than information presented in a continuous paragraph. Presenting information in a list not only improves the content structure, but also improves its readability. By using the various list options in Word, you can create well-structured documents.

Lists

Definition:

A *list* is a data grouping method in which the items in a group are displayed one after the other. A list often has a lead-in sentence that provides a brief description about the items in it. There can be any number of items in a list. Lists can be created in a single or multiple level and can use various styles of numbers or bullets.

Example:

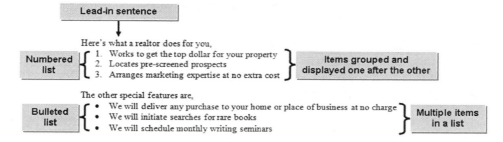

Figure 3-6: The two list types available in Word.

Bulleted and Numbered Lists

There are two main types of lists in Word that allow you to group items according to your preferences.

List Type	Used To
Numbered (Ordered)	Denote a ranking among items, a sequence that must be followed, or a count of items. You can customize the list by choosing different alphabetic or number formats such as numeric or Roman. *Numbered lists* can be multi-level, and the items in a list may be a word, short phrase, or paragraph.
Bulleted (Unordered)	Denote a group of equally significant items. They are grouped under the same heading. You can customize the list by choosing different bullet styles. *Bulleted lists* can be multi-level. Each bulleted item in a list may be a word, short phrase, or paragraph.

How to Display Text as List Items

Procedure Reference: Apply Bullets to Existing Text

To apply bullets to existing text:

1. Select the paragraphs that you want to transform to a list.
2. Create the list.
    *   On the **Home** tab, in the **Paragraph** group, click the **Bullets** button to create a bulleted list or;
    *   On the **Home** tab, in the **Paragraph** group, click the **Numbering** button, to create a numbered list.
3. Specify the bullet or numbering format.
    *   Select the symbol format for a bulleted list or;
        *   On the **Home** tab, in the **Paragraph** group, click the **Bullets** drop-down arrow, and from the **Bullets Library,** select the desired bullet format or;
        *   Right-click the selected text, and choose **Bullets,** and select the desired bullet format.
    *   Select the desired numbering format for a numbered list.
        *   On the **Home** tab, in the **Paragraph** group, click the **Numbering** drop-down arrow, and from the **Numbering Library,** select the desired numbering format or;
        *   Right-click the selected text, and choose **Numbering,** and select the desired numbering format.

Procedure Reference: Create a List

To create a list:

1. Place the insertion point where you want to start a list.
2. On the **Home** tab, in the **Paragraph** group, select the desired list type.
3. Type the first list item and press **Enter.**
4. If necessary, add more items to the list.
5. Press **Enter** twice or click the appropriate list button again to end the list.

Procedure Reference: Remove Bullets and Numbering

To remove bullets and numbering:

1. Select the desired list.
2. On the **Home** tab, in the **Paragraph** group, click the appropriate button.
    *   Click the **Bullets** button to remove the bullets.
    *   Click the **Numbering** button to remove the numbering.

Procedure Reference: Define a New Bullet

To define a new bullet:

1. On the **Home** tab, in the **Paragraph** group, from the **Bullets** drop-down list, select **Define New Bullet** to display the **Define New Bullet** dialog box.

2. In the **Define New Bullet** dialog box, in the **Bullet character** section, select the desired bullet character.

3. In the **Alignment** section, from the drop-down list, select the desired style of alignment.

4. In the **Preview** text box, preview the bullet.

5. Click **OK** to close the **Define New Bullet** dialog box.

Procedure Reference: Define a New Number Format

To define a new number format:

1. On the **Home** tab, in the **Paragraph** group, from the **Numbering** drop-down list, select **Define New Number Format** to display the **Define New Number Format** dialog box.

2. In the **Define New Number Format** dialog box, in the **Number style** section, select the desired numbering style.

3. In the **Alignment** section, from the drop-down list, select the desired style of alignment.

4. In the **Preview** text box, preview the numbering format.

5. Click **OK** to close the **Define New Number Format** dialog box.

Customizing the List Formats

You can either create a customized list or change the format of a list. Right-click the list, and from the displayed menu, choose either **Bullets** to see the bullet formats or **Numbering** to see the various numbering formats. Click **Define New Bullet** or **Define New Number Format** to create custom lists.

The AutoFormat As You Type Option

When you want to start a new list, you can use the **AutoFormat As You Type** option in Word. To start a bulleted list, type an asterisk (*), press **Tab,** type the list item, and press **Enter.** Word will convert the asterisk into a bullet and begin a bulleted list for you.

To start a numbered list, type the first number of the list and any trailing punctuation such as a period or an open parentheses, press **Tab,** type the list item, and press **Enter.** Again, Word will begin the numbered list by using the numbering format you want. You can use the **AutoCorrect** dialog box to control these automatic list settings.

ACTIVITY 3-4
Creating Numbered and Bulleted Lists

Before You Begin:
The My OGC Properties.docx file is open.

Scenario:
You feel that the information about the functioning of realtors could be presented in a better way if they were listed out. You also want to present the disclaimer content in a clear and concise manner, so that the readers can have a better understanding of it.

1. Format a paragraph as a numbered list.

   a. Scroll up to display the bottom of the first page.

   b. Under the title "Selling Your Home," click before the text "Works," hold down **Shift,** and click after the paragraph mark at the end of the text "buyer."

   c. On the **Home** tab, in the **Paragraph** group, click the **Numbering** button to convert the selected text to a numbered list.

2. Add a sixth item to the list.

   a. At the end of the numbered list, place the insertion point after the text "for the buyer."

   b. Press **Enter** to start a new list item.

   c. Type ***Ensures that there are no surprises at closing***

3. Format a paragraph as a bulleted list.

   a. Scroll down to display the top of the second page and select the content below the heading "Disclaimer."

   b. On the **Home** tab, in the **Paragraph** group, click the **Bullets** button to convert the text to a bulleted list and save the document.

TOPIC D
Modify the Layout of a Paragraph

You displayed text in the form of list items. You can also set paragraph formatting to control the layout of the paragraph as a whole. In this topic, you will modify the paragraph layouts in a Word document.

Paragraph layout options give you a great deal of control over the appearance of a paragraph on a page. By making the appropriate paragraph layout choices, you can add variety and a professionally published look to your Word documents.

Margins

Definition:

A *margin* is the blank area that surrounds text along the top, bottom, left, and right edges of a page. Margins not only determine the overall size of a document's text area in relation to the size of the paper it will print on, but also the text's vertical or horizontal position on a page. Margins can also affect other layout options, which may be set in relation to the size of the margins.

Example:

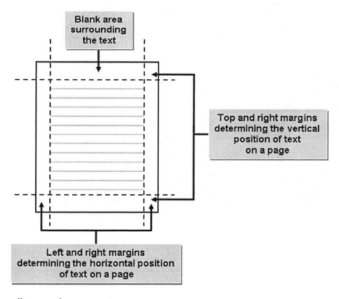

Figure 3-7: Margins surrounding a document.

Paragraph Alignment Options

The *paragraph alignment* options in Word determine how a paragraph will be horizontally positioned between the left and the right margins in a document.

Option	Description
Align Text Left	Aligns the left edge of a paragraph along the left margin. The paragraph's right edge appears jagged.
Center	Aligns both sides of a paragraph equidistant from left and right margins. Both left and right edges of the paragraph appear jagged.
Align Text Right	Aligns the right edge of a paragraph along the right margin. The paragraph's left edge appears jagged.
Justify	Aligns both sides of a paragraph along the left and right margins. The paragraph's left and right edges do not appear jagged. Word adjusts the spacing between the words so that they stretch from the left margin to the right margin.

Indents

Definition:

An *indent* enables you to independently align the left and right edges of a paragraph from the margins of a document. Indents, which are either positive or negative, affect only the paragraphs that are selected. A positive indent allows you to make the width of a paragraph narrower than the margin on one or both sides, while a negative indent allows you to make the width of the paragraph extend past the margin on one or both sides.

> Another word for a negative indent is an outdent because it makes the paragraph extend out into the margin space.

Example:

Figure 3-8: Different types of indentation applied to a text.

Indent Markers

You can set the indentation for an active paragraph by dragging any of the four indent markers that are available at the edges of the horizontal ruler of a Word document.

Indent Marker	Description
First Line	Controls the left boundary of the first line of a paragraph.
Hanging	Controls the left boundary of every line in a paragraph, except the first line. This is generally used to align the first line with the margin and indent the remainder of the paragraph away from the margin.
Left	Controls the left boundary of every line in a paragraph.
Right	Controls the right boundary of every line in a paragraph.

Using Indents for Quoted Materials

A standard way to format a lengthy section of a quoted material within a document is to place it within a paragraph that is indented on both sides.

Indentation Options

The indentation options in the **Paragraph** dialog box allow you to place indents on the ruler, with an accuracy of 0.1 inch.

Option	Description
Left Indent	Displays the current left indentation that is applied to a paragraph. You can either click the spin box to increase or decrease the indentation value or just type the value in the **Left** text box.

Option	Description
Right Indent	Displays the current right indentation that is applied to a paragraph. You can either click the spin box to increase or decrease the indentation value or just type the value in the **Right** text box.
Special Indent	Displays whether a **First Line** or **Hanging** indent marker is set for the selected paragraph.
By	Displays the amount of indentation for the special indent in the selected paragraph.
Mirror indents	Enables you to set the **Inside** and **Outside** indents for a paragraph. When the paragraph is moved from a left page to right page or vice-versa, the left and right indents are swapped automatically.

Spacing Options

The spacing options in the **Paragraph** dialog box allow you to customize the amount of spacing between lines and paragraphs.

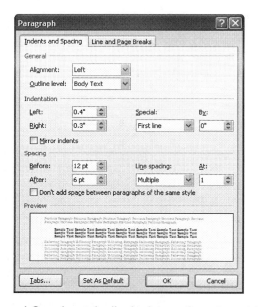

Figure 3-9: The Indents and Spacing tab displaying options to set indents.

Option	Description
Before	Allows you to specify the amount of space before the selected paragraph. The spacing before a paragraph can vary from 0 to 1584 points.
After	Allows you to specify the amount of space after the selected paragraph. The spacing after a paragraph can vary from 0 to 1584 points.
Line spacing	Allows you to specify the amount of space between the lines in a paragraph. You can set single space, one and a half space, or double space. You can also set the spacing to an exact or a minimum amount, or choose **Multiple** to adjust the spacing by a percentage of the existing spacing.

Option	Description
At	Allows you to specify the amount of space between the lines in the selected text. The value entered in this field depends on the **Line spacing** option that is selected.
Don't add space between para- graphs of the same style	Does not allow you to add any space between paragraphs that have the same style.

Hyphenation

The hyphenation feature in Word allows you to insert hyphens to split words across lines. This allows you to maintain an even line length and eliminate unwanted gaps in text. You can insert an optional hyphen or a non-breaking hyphen. Hyphenation options can be accessed from the **Page Setup** group on the **Page Layout** tab.

A number of options are available in the **Hyphenation** drop-down list.

Options	Description
None	Allows you to disable the hyphenation option in the document.
Automatic	Instructs Word to automatically hyphenate the document.
Manual	Allows you to manually hyphenate the words in a document .
Hyphenation Options	Allows you to change the options available in the **Hyphenation Options** dialog box.

Non-breaking spaces

When Word calculates the width of a line and wraps the text with the next line, it breaks the line either at a place where there is space or at a place where there is a hyphen. At times you may not want to break the line at a certain place. By inserting non-breaking spaces, you can retain words on the same line.

How to Modify the Layout of a Paragraph

Procedure Reference: Control the Layout of a Paragraph

To control the layout of a paragraph:

1. Select the paragraph or paragraphs that you want to adjust.

 If you want to change the alignment for only one paragraph, rather than selecting that paragraph, you can just place the insertion point in it.

2. Apply the desired paragraph alignment.

   ● On the **Home** tab, in the **Paragraph** group, select the desired alignment or;

   ● Open the **Paragraph** dialog box, and from the **Alignment** drop-down list, select the desired alignment, and click **OK.**

3. Set the indent.

   ● On the **Home** tab, in the **Paragraph** group, click the **Increase Indent** or **Decrease Indent** button to indent the left edge of the paragraph by 0.5 inches to the right or left or;

 The **Increase Indent** and **Decrease Indent** buttons do not affect the first line, hanging, or right indent.

   ● On the horizontal ruler, drag the appropriate indent markers to a new position to make quick adjustments or;

   ● Open the **Paragraph** dialog box, change the **Indentation** settings and click **OK.**

 The **Paragraph** dialog box provides the most accurate way to change the indentation settings. You can configure a value to an accuracy of 0.1 inches.

4. Set the spacing between the lines in the paragraph.

   ● On the **Home** tab, in the **Paragraph** group, from the **Line and Paragraph Spacing** drop-down list, from the list of fixed spacing values, select the desired amount of line spacing or;

   ● Open the **Paragraph** dialog box, and in the **Spacing** section, select a line spacing option. If you select **At least, Exactly,** or **Multiple,** from the **Line Spacing** drop-down list, type the spacing value in the **At** spin box and click **OK.**

5. In the **Paragraph** dialog box, in the **Spacing** section, in the **Before** and **After** spin boxes, specify the amount of space to be set before and after a paragraph.

Procedure Reference: Set Hyphenation Options

To set the hyphenation options:

1. Open the document in which hyphenation needs to be applied.

2. On the **Page Layout** tab, in the **Page Setup** group, from the **Hyphenation** drop-down list, select an option.

3. If necessary, in the **Hyphenation** dialog box set more options for hyphenating.

    a. From the **Hyphenation** drop-down list, select **Hyphenation Options.**

    b. In the **Hyphenation** dialog box, set the desired options.

- Check the **Automatically hyphenate document** check box to hyphenate the document automatically.

- Check the **Hyphenate words in CAPS** check box to allow hyphenation of words which are capitalized.

- In the **Hyphenation zone** spin box, set a value to define the number of characters that hyphenated words are allowed to be split into or;

- In the **Limit consecutive hyphens to** spin box, set a value to limit the number of consecutive lines that can contain hyphenated words.

    c. Click **OK** to close the **Hyphenation** dialog box.

Procedure Reference: Apply First Line and Hanging Indents

To apply first line and hanging indents:

1. On the **Home** tab, in the **Paragraph** group, click the **Paragraph** dialog box launcher.

2. In the **Paragraph** dialog box, in the **Indentation** section, from the **Special** drop-down list, select an indentation option.

- Select **First line** to indent only the first line of text in a paragraph.

- Select **Hanging** to indent all the lines in a paragraph except the first line or;

- Select **none** to remove all indents.

3. In the **By** spin box, set the extent to which you want to indent the text in a paragraph.

4. Close the **Paragraph** dialog box.

ACTIVITY 3-5
Aligning Paragraphs

Before You Begin:

The My OGC Properties.docx file is open.

Scenario:

You want to proofread the sales details that you have prepared before presenting the information to the managers. During the review, you notice that the title is not in the center and that the quarterly data is not easily distinguishable from the rest of the text. Moreover, the disclaimer text blends in with the rest of the content and the paragraphs are not appropriately spaced to enable your colleagues to make notes during the meeting. You decide to ensure that the document is easily readable and neatly presented.

---

1. Align the title to the center of the document.

   a. Scroll up to the top of the document and select the text from "OGC PROPERTIES, INC." through "property for you!"

   b. On the **Home** tab, in the **Paragraph** group, click the **Center** button to center align the title.

---

2. Center align the headings above the tabbed data.

   a. Scroll down to the top of the second page and select the text from "Houses Sold" through "Housing Units."

   b. On the **Home** tab, in the **Paragraph** group, click the **Center** button.

---

3. Set the indents for the disclaimer text.

   a. If necessary, scroll down to view the "Disclaimer" paragraph.

   b. In the document, select the "Disclaimer" heading along with the three points in the bulleted list below it.

c. On the **Home** tab, in the **Paragraph** group, in the first row, click the **Increase Indent** button to increase the indent by 0.5 inches.

d. On the horizontal ruler, drag the **Right Indent** marker to the 5-inch mark.

e. Under the heading "Disclaimer," select the text from "Errors" through "imply an endorsement" and the paragraph formatting mark after it.

f. On the horizontal ruler, drag the **First Line Indent** marker, which is the inverted triangle, by a quarter of an inch to the right.

4. Add six points of space before the sales data title.

   a. Above the sales data, place the insertion point before the text "First Quarter Data."

   b. On the **Home** tab, in the **Paragraph** group, click the **Paragraph** dialog box launcher.

   c. In the **Paragraph** dialog box, in the **Spacing** section, in the **Before** spin box, click the up arrow to change the spacing to **6 pt.**

   d. Click **OK** to apply the spacing and to close the dialog box.

5. Add six points of space between the bullet points in the disclaimer.

   a. Select the three bullet points below the heading "Disclaimer."

    b.   On the **Home** tab, in the **Paragraph** group, click the **Paragraph** dialog box launcher.

    c.   In the **Paragraph** dialog box, in the **Spacing** section, in the **After** spin box, click the up arrow to change the spacing to **6 pt.**

    d.   Uncheck the **Don't add space between paragraphs of the same style** check box.

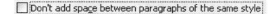

    e.   Click **OK** to apply spacing and to close the dialog box.

6.   Apply line spacing to sales data.

    a.   Select the sales data including the header line and the three lines of data and the text "Source: OGC Properties."

    b.   In the **Paragraph** group, from the **Line and Paragraph Spacing** drop-down list, select **1.5** to increase the space between the list items.

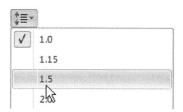

    c.   Click after the text "Source: OGC Properties" to deselect the text.

    d.   Save the document.

TOPIC E
Apply Styles

You modified the layout of paragraphs in a Word document. At times, you may want to reuse the formatting across documents, or apply several formatting options consistently to the paragraphs in a single document. In this topic, you will apply styles to text in a Word document.

When creating official documents, you may want to apply specific design and typographical changes to them. Instead of accessing options from different dialog boxes, Word provides a way for you to apply the desired style using predefined style galleries. Applying styles helps you quickly achieve consistent design and text formatting throughout a document.

Word Styles

Definition:

A *Word style* is a collection of appearance settings that can be applied to sections of a document as a group. Using a style can be quicker than applying individual formatting options, and it can ensure consistency of formatting throughout a document. A style may include text formatting options, such as different font typefaces, colors, and effects, and paragraph formatting options, such as line spacing, borders, and shading. You can use built-in styles, modify existing styles, or create custom styles.

Example:

Figure 3-10: Different Font Styles applied to a text.

Quick Style Sets

A *Quick Style set* is a package of styles that work well together when applied to a document as a group. By changing from one Quick Style set to another, you can apply design and formatting changes to a document all at the same time, by switching from the styles in one set to their equivalents in another set. The styles in the current Quick Style set are displayed in the **Styles** group of the **Home** tab. You can scroll to select a style or click the **More** button to view the Styles gallery. Word includes several predefined Quick Style sets. You can also build a new style set or modify an existing style set and then add it to the Quick Styles gallery.

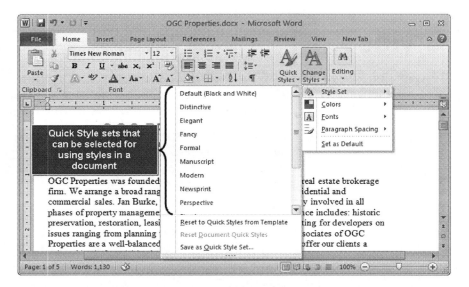

Figure 3-11: *The Quick Styles Set gallery displaying the default style sets available in Word.*

Changing a Quick Style Set

If you want to change to a different Quick Style set, click the **Change Styles** button in the **Styles** group, choose **Style Set,** and then select the desired style set. You can move the mouse pointer over each style set name to see a live preview of how the text will look in that style set. When you choose a set, all the styles in the document will update to the equivalent styles in the new style set. For example, if you have applied the **Heading 1** style from the default Quick Style set, when you change to a different set, the **Heading 1** style in the new set will be applied to all the **Heading 1** text in the document.

The Styles Task Pane

The **Styles** task pane contains various options that help you work with styles.

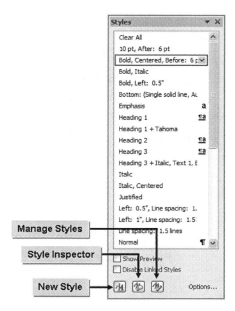

Figure 3-12: The Styles task pane displaying the various styles and options to work with styles.

Option	Description
Clear All	Clears all the styles that were applied to the selected text.
Show Preview	Shows a preview of the styles.
Disable Linked Styles	Disables the styles that can be applied to both paragraphs and individual characters.
New Style	Opens the **Create New Style from Formatting** dialog box, where you can create a new style and add it to the styles list.
Style Inspector	Opens the **Style Inspector** task pane, where you can customize the formatting for a paragraph or text that you have selected.
Manage Styles	Opens the **Manage Styles** dialog box that contains tabs with options to edit, recommend, restrict, and set default styles.
Options	Opens the **Style Pane Options** dialog box, where you can customize the **Styles** gallery.

The Apply Styles Task Pane

The **Apply Styles** task pane is used to modify or reapply a style that is already applied to a document. It can be invoked by pressing **Ctrl+Shift+S.** It can also be invoked by selecting the **Home** tab and clicking the **More** button in the **Styles** group and choosing **Apply Styles.**

The Style Inspector Task Pane

The **Style Inspector** task pane allows you to determine whether the current formatting is applied completely through a style, or whether direct formatting is in effect. It can be used to clear formatting at a paragraph or character level. This task pane can be displayed by clicking the **Style Inspector** button in the **Styles** task pane.

How to Apply Styles

Procedure Reference: Apply a Style

To apply a style:

1.   Select the text to which you want to apply a style.
2.   Apply the desired style to the selected text.

  ● On the **Home** tab, in the **Styles** group, select a style, or click the **More** button and select the desired style from the **Styles** gallery or;

  ● On the **Home** tab, in the **Styles** group, click the **Styles** dialog box launcher, and in the **Styles** task pane, select the desired style.

ACTIVITY 3-6
Applying Styles

Before You Begin:
The My OGC Properties.docx file is open.

Scenario:
You want to enhance the visual appeal of the document you are working on. Your manager has also approved the contents in the document and has asked you to ensure that the title and headings in the document are distinct. In order to draw the attention of the readers on the company's affiliations, you decide to highlight the text conveying this information.

---

1. Apply the **Heading 1** style to the titles in the first page.

   a. Scroll up to the beginning of the document and click before the title "About Us."

   b. On the **Home** tab, in the **Styles** group, from the displayed gallery, select **Heading 1.**

   c. Scroll down and select the titles "Description of Our Firm," "Our Corporate Philosophy," and "Our Goal."

   d. On the **Home** tab, in the **Styles** group, from the displayed gallery, select **Heading 1.**

---

2. Apply the **Title** style to the title "Locations."

   a. Scroll down to display the top of the fourth page of the document and place the insertion point at the beginning of the title "Locations."

   b. On the **Home** tab, in the **Styles** group, click the **More** button, and from the displayed gallery, select the **Title** style.

---

3. Apply the **Intense Emphasis** style to the affiliations.

   a. Scroll up to the third page and in the paragraph under the title "Our Company Affiliations," select the text "Association of Realtors" through "National Referral Roster (NRR)."

b. On the **Home** tab, in the **Styles** group, click the **More** button, and from the displayed gallery, select the **Intense Emphasis** style, which is the first style in the third row.

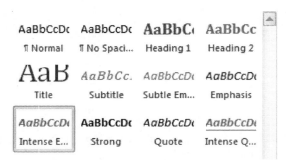

c. Click anywhere in the text area to deselect the text and then save the document.

TOPIC F

Manage Formatting

You applied styles to the text in a Word document. Once you have completed all your formatting, you might want to copy, delete, or replace some of it. In this topic, you will manage formatting in a Word document.

When working with documents that have complex text formatting, you may need to locate specific instances of formatting, apply formatting from one paragraph or section to another, or remove the formatting. It can be tedious to manually scan a document and make the formatting changes. Word provides various tools that you can use to efficiently find and replace complex formatting.

The Reveal Formatting Task Pane

The options in the **Reveal Formatting** task pane help you identify specific formatting options that are applied to a text selection, including fonts, alignment, indents, document margins, and layouts. This task pane also lets you compare the formatting of one section to that of another, select text with similar formatting, and apply or clear formatting.

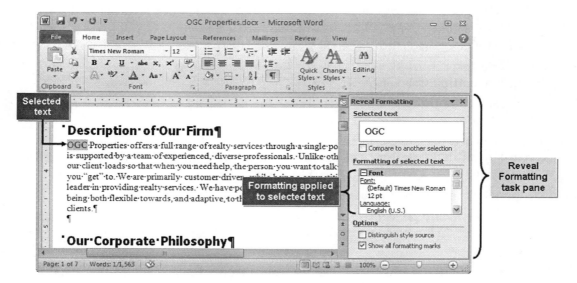

Figure 3-13: The Reveal Formatting task pane displaying the formatting applied to selected text.

Clear Formatting Options

You can clear the formatting in a selection and reset the selection's appearance to the default format by using the **Reveal Formatting** task pane, the **Styles** task pane, the **Style Inspector** task pane, or the **Clear Formatting** button on the **Home** tab in the **Font** group.

Find and Replace Text Formatting Options

You can find all the instances where you have applied a particular format or replace one set of format options with another by using the **Find and Replace** text formatting options. You can use the **Format** drop-down list in the **Find and Replace** dialog box to search for a specific format option and replace it with a desired format. You can search for, and replace, character and paragraph formatting, tabs and tab settings, styles, highlighting, and other formatting options.

How to Manage Formatting

Procedure Reference: Manage Formatting Using the Reveal Formatting Task Pane

To manage formatting using the **Reveal Formatting** task pane:

1. On the **Home** tab, in the **Styles** group, click the **Styles** dialog box launcher to display the **Styles** task pane.
2. In the **Styles** task pane, click the **Style Inspector** button.
3. In the **Style Inspector** task pane, click the **Reveal Formatting** button to display the **Reveal Formatting** task pane.
4. If necessary, close the **Styles** and **Style Inspector** task panes to show more of the document window.
5. In the document, select the desired text to reveal the text formatting applied to it. The **Reveal Formatting** task pane will display the details of both the font and paragraph formatting options that are applied.
6. Perform the desired format management task.
   - Move the mouse pointer over the **Selected text** text box, click the drop-down arrow, and choose **Clear Formatting** to clear the font and paragraph formatting applied to the selection.
   - From the **Selected text** drop-down list, select **Apply Formatting of Surrounding Text** to make the format of the selection match the format of the text around it.
   - From the **Selected text** drop-down list, select **Select All Text With Similar Formatting** to select other text in the document with similar formatting.
   - Check the **Compare to another selection** check box and select the second portion of the text in the document to compare the formatting of two selections.
7. Close the **Reveal Formatting** task pane.

Procedure Reference: Clear Formatting

To clear formatting:

1. Select the text that contains the formatting you want to clear.

2. Clear the desired formatting.

    - Open the **Styles** task pane and click the **Clear All** button or;
    - Open the **Style Inspector** task pane and click **Clear All** or;
    - Open the **Style Inspector** task pane and click the **Clear Paragraph Formatting** or **Clear Character Formatting** button.
    - On the **Home** tab in the **Font** group, click the **Clear Formatting** button.
    - Open the **Reveal Formatting** task pane, and from the **Selected text** drop-down list, select **Clear Formatting.**

Procedure Reference: Find and Replace Formatting

To find and replace formatting in a document:

1. Click at the beginning of a document.
2. On the **Home** tab, in the **Editing** group, click the **Replace** button.
3. In the **Find and Replace** dialog box, in the **Find what** text box, delete any unwanted text and formatting options.
4. Set the find formatting options.

    a. Click the **More** button, and in the **Replace** section, from the **Format** drop-down list, select the desired attribute.

    b. In the **Find <attribute>** dialog box, select the attributes that you want to find and click **OK.**

5. In the **Replace with** text box, delete the unwanted text and formatting options.
6. Set the replace formatting options.

    a. Click the **More** button, and in the **Replace** section, select the desired attribute.

    b. In the **Replace <attribute>** dialog box, select the attributes that you want to replace instead of the existing attribute and click **OK.**

7. Replace occurrences of the formatting applied to text, as needed.
8. In the **Microsoft Word** message box, click **OK.**
9. Close the **Find and Replace** dialog box.

Removing Formats from a Prior Search

When you display the **Replace** tab in the **Find and Replace** dialog box, some font formats may already be displayed in the **Find what** and **Replace with** text boxes, perhaps left over from a previous task. Before you begin a new search, you should remove the formats so that they do not interfere with the new search. To remove the formats from the **Find** or **Replace** tab of the **Find and Replace** dialog box, click **More** to display the **Search** and **Replace** options and click the **No Formatting** button.

ACTIVITY 3-7
Clearing Text Formatting

Before You Begin:

The My OGC Properties.docx file is open.

Scenario:

You enhanced the visual appeal of a document by applying different styles to it. Upon reviewing the document, you find that you are distracted by formatting inconsistencies and are not able to focus on the main points. You decide to remove such formatting to ensure that readers stay focused on the content.

---

1. Determine the existing formatting for the text "unconditionally guarantee."

    a. Scroll down to the fourth page and below the title "Our Guarantee," select the text "unconditionally guarantee."

    b. On the **Home** tab, in the **Styles** group, click the **Styles** dialog box launcher.

    c. In the **Styles** task pane, click the **Style Inspector** button.

    d. Close the **Styles** task pane.

    e. In the **Style Inspector** task pane, click the **Reveal Formatting** button to display the **Reveal Formatting** task pane.

    f. Close the **Style Inspector** task pane.

    g. In the **Reveal Formatting** task pane, observe that the font attributes include the **Times New Roman** font, **12 pt,** and **Italic.**

2. Clear the Italic font attribute from the text "unconditionally guarantee."

    a. In the **Reveal Formatting** task pane, move the mouse pointer over the **Selected text** text box to reveal the drop-down arrow.

    b. From the **Selected text** drop-down list, select **Apply Formatting of Surrounding Text** to clear the italic font attribute, but retain the font type and size.

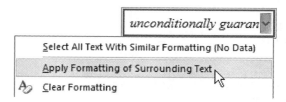

    c. Close the **Reveal Formatting** task pane and save the document.

ACTIVITY 3-8
Finding and Replacing Text Formatting

Before You Begin:

The My OGC Properties.docx file is open.

Scenario:

Your company report is ready for your manager's review. Before you submit it for review, you get to know that Tahoma is the font style that is normally used in all the official company documents. To maintain consistency, you decide to change all occurrences of the Arial font with Tahoma.

1. Set Arial as the font to be searched for.

    a. Place the insertion point at the beginning of the document.

    b. On the **Home** tab, in the **Editing** group, click **Replace.**

    c. In the **Find and Replace** dialog box, on the **Replace** tab, click **More.**

    d. In the **Replace** section, from the **Format** drop-down list, select **Font.**

    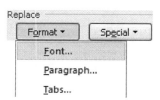

    e. In the **Find Font** dialog box, in the **Font** list box, if necessary, scroll down and select **Arial** and click **OK.**

    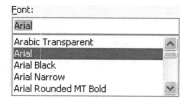

2. Set Tahoma as the replacement font.

    a. In the **Find and Replace** dialog box, click in the **Replace with** text box.

b.   In the **Replace** section, from the **Format** drop-down list, select **Font.**

c.   In the **Replace Font** dialog box, in the **Font** list box, scroll down and select **Tahoma** and then click **OK.**

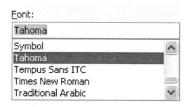

d.   Click **Less** to close the advanced options.

3.   Replace all instances of Arial with Tahoma.

a.   In the **Find and Replace** dialog box, click **Replace All.**

b.   In the **Microsoft Word** message box, observe the message that Word has completed searching the document and replaced all instances with the necessary changes and click **OK.**

4.   Clear the font formats in the **Find and Replace** dialog box.

a.   In the **Find and Replace** dialog box, verify that the insertion point is in the **Find what** text box.

b.   Click **More** to display the advanced options, and in the **Replace** section, click **No Formatting.**

c.   Click in the **Replace with** text box, and in the **Replace** section, click **No Formatting.**

d.   Click **Close.**

e.   Save the document.

TOPIC G
Apply Borders and Shading

You managed the formatting applied to text in a Word document. In addition to formatting text, you may now want to ensure that critical paragraphs are highlighted to be distinguished from the rest of the content on a page. In this topic, you will apply borders and shading to paragraphs.

Shaded paragraphs and borders draw attention to the content and help readers quickly locate the key sections of a Word document. This ensures that readers who skim the document do not miss out on any important information.

Borders

Definition:

A *border* is a decorative line or pattern that is displayed around objects. There are different types of borders that can be applied to paragraphs, pages, and pictures to draw attention to them. Borders help you present data by aligning the text on a page. Borders can be applied to the top, bottom, or all four sides of a page or an object.

Example:

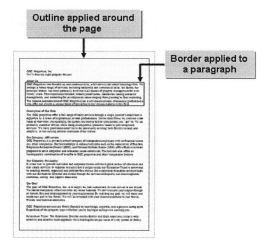

Figure 3-14: Border applied to a page in a document.

Types of Borders

You can view a list of predefined border types in the **Border** drop-down list in the **Paragraph** group on the **Home** tab.

Border Type	Description
Bottom Border	Inserts a line below the selected object or text.
Top Border	Inserts a line above the selected object or text.
Left Border	Inserts a line to the left of the selected object or text.
Right Border	Inserts a line to the right of the selected object or text.
No Border	Removes the existing border from the selected object or text.
All Borders	Applies an outline to the table that is selected and inserts vertical and horizontal lines between the table cells. This option works only on tables.
Outside Borders	Applies an outline to the selected object.
Inside Borders	Inserts vertical and horizontal lines between the table cells. This option works only on tables.
Inside Horizontal Border	Inserts horizontal lines between the selected rows of a table. This option works only on tables.
Inside Vertical Border	Inserts vertical lines between the selected columns of a table. This option works only on tables.
Diagonal Down Border	Inserts a descending diagonal line across a selected cell. This option works only on tables.
Diagonal Up Border	Inserts an ascending diagonal line across a selected cell. This option works only on tables.

Additional Border Options

In addition to directly selecting a predefined border, there are options in the **Border** drop-down list that allow users to customize and specify how the borders are to be displayed in a document.

Border Option	Description
Horizontal Line	Inserts a horizontal line on the line where the insertion point is placed.
Draw Table	Draws a table of the desired size.
View Gridlines	Shows or hides the gridlines in tables.
Borders and Shading	Opens the **Borders and Shading** dialog box.

Shading

Definition:

Shading is a percentage of color that can be added to the background of objects. Shading can be used to highlight information in a document or to apply a shadow effect. You can apply shading to a line, paragraph, or table data. You can specify a plain fill color, or a pattern in a contrasting color.

Example:

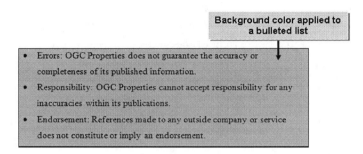

Figure 3-15: Shading applied to highlight important content.

The Borders and Shading Dialog Box

The **Borders and Shading** dialog box has three tabs that allow you to specify the exact kind of border or coloring that you want to apply to the selected objects.

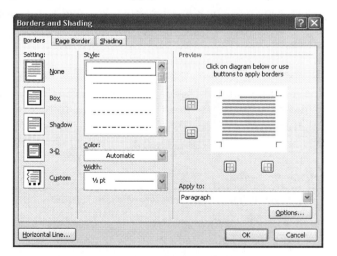

Figure 3-16: The Borders and Shading dialog box displaying the border options on the Borders tab.

Tab	Allows You To
Borders	Specify the type of border, its style, color, width, and the object to which it should be applied. It also shows a preview of the options that you set.
Page Border	Specify the type of page border, its style, color, width, art, and object to which it should be applied. It also shows a preview of the options that you set.

Tab	Allows You To
Shading	Specify the fill color, the pattern and pattern color, and the object to which it should be applied. It also shows a preview of the options that you set.

How to Apply Borders and Shading

Procedure Reference: Add a Border or Shading

To add a border or shading:

1. Select the paragraph or paragraphs to which you want to add a border or shading.
2. Apply the border.
   - On the **Home** tab, in the **Paragraph** group, from the Border drop-down list, select an existing border type to apply a predefined border or;
   - Select the desired settings.
     a. From the Border drop-down list, select **Borders and Shading** to open the **Borders and Shading** dialog box.
     b. In the **Borders and Shading** dialog box, on the **Borders** tab, in the **Setting** section, select the desired settings.
     c. Click **OK** to close the **Borders and Shading** dialog box.
3. Add the shading.
   - Apply shading using the **Borders and Shading** dialog box.
     a. Open the **Borders and Shading** dialog box and select the **Shading** tab.
     b. From the **Fill** drop-down list, select a color to add an overall fill color.
     c. If necessary, from the **Style** drop-down list, select the shading percentage or pattern.
     d. If necessary, from the **Color** drop-down list, select a color for the pattern.
     e. Click **OK** to apply the shading and close the dialog box.
   - On the **Home** tab, in the **Paragraph** group, from the **Shading** drop-down list, select the desired color to add only a fill color.
4. If necessary, from the **Shading** drop-down list, select **No Color** to remove the shading.

ACTIVITY 3-9
Applying Borders and Shading to a Paragraph

Before You Begin:

The My OGC Properties.docx file is open.

Scenario:

In the document that you created, you have the sales data of your company. Since you have lot of contents in the document, you feel that the regional managers might loose track of the sales data. So you decide to structure and highlight the sales data to draw their attention. You also feel that the disclaimer information needs to be prominently visible because it is of prime importance to clients.

---

1. Apply the top and bottom borders for the tabbed text.

    a. Scroll to the top of the second page of the document and, click the blank line above the title "Houses Sold by Region."

    b. On the **Home** tab, in the **Paragraph** group, in the Borders drop-down list, verify that **Bottom Border** is selected, and click the Borders button.

    c. Click the blank line below the text "Source: OGC Properties."

    d. On the **Home** tab, in the **Paragraph** group, from the Borders drop-down list, select **Top Border.**

---

2. Select a box border for the disclaimer text.

    a. In the document, below the heading "Disclaimer," select the three bullet points.

b.   On the **Home** tab, in the **Paragraph** group, from the Borders drop-down list, select
Borders and Shading.

c.   In the **Borders and Shading** dialog box, on the **Borders** tab, in the **Setting** section,
select **Box,** and from the **Width** drop-down list, select **1½ pt.**

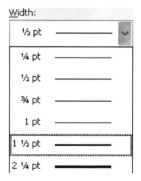

    d.   Observe that the border resulting from the selected settings is displayed in the **Preview** section.

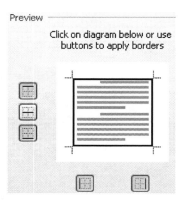

3.   Apply the orange background color to the disclaimer text.

    a.   In the **Borders and Shading** dialog box, select the **Shading** tab.

    b.   On the **Shading** tab, from the **Fill** drop-down list, in the **Standard Colors** section, select **Orange,** which is the third color from the left, and click **OK** to apply the shading and to close the **Borders and Shading** dialog box.

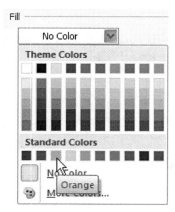

    c.   Click anywhere on the page to deselect the text.

    d.   Save and close the document.

Lesson 3 Follow-up

In this lesson, you modified the appearance of text in a Word document. By properly formatting text and paragraphs in a document, you can reduce the reading effort for your audience.

1. **Which text formatting options do you expect to use most often in your Word documents?**

2. **When formatting documents, which Word tools will you find most helpful?**

4 | Inserting Special Characters and Graphical Objects

Lesson Time: 30 minutes

Lesson Objectives:

In this lesson, you will insert special characters and graphical objects.

You will:

* Insert symbols and special characters.
* Add illustrations to a document.

Introduction

You modified the appearance of text in Word 2010. You can also improve the presentation of content by including visual elements in a document. In this lesson, you will insert special characters and graphical objects.

While creating documents, it may be necessary to add certain special characters to provide clarity to the content. Also, when you create a lengthy document with just text, it can be difficult to assimilate content. Looking at only text, readers may lose interest, and eventually, the document may not serve its purpose. By inserting graphical objects, you can engage readers as well as ensure better comprehension of the content.

TOPIC A

Insert Symbols and Special Characters

You used various formatting techniques to enhance the appearance of text in a document. However, sometimes you may not be able to bring clarity to your content without the use of symbols such as the copyright symbol (©). In this topic, you will insert symbols and special characters in a Word document.

You are drafting a copyright statement and the new department style guide requires that you use the copyright symbol (©) along with the word "copyright." You've stared at your keyboard for several minutes trying to locate the character, but it is nowhere to be found. How are you going to get the circle around the letter "c"? You know it can be done, but how? Word provides convenient access to a large group of symbols and special characters such as the copyright symbol, which can be inserted easily.

Symbols

Definition:

Symbols are character marks that can be used to represent an idea or a word such as copyright, trademark, or registered trademark. Symbols are included with every font. However, each font can have a different set of symbols. Symbols can include pictorial representations, icons, mathematical and scientific notations, and characters from the alphabet of other languages.

Example:

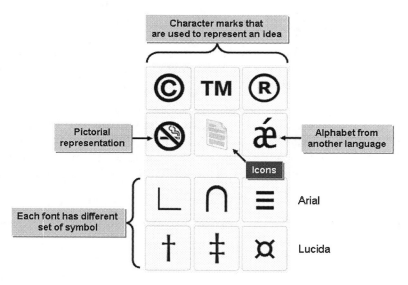

Figure 4-1: *Different symbols available for use in Word documents.*

Special Characters

Definition:

Special characters are punctuation, spacing, or typographical characters that typically are not available on a standard keyboard. Some of the special characters can be obtained with a key combination of ALT and other keys on the keyboard.

Example:

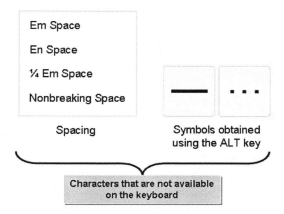

Figure 4-2: *Special characters that can be inserted in Word documents.*

How to Insert Symbols and Special Characters

Procedure Reference: Insert a Symbol or Special Character.

To insert a symbol or special character:

1. Place the insertion point where you want to insert a symbol or special character.
2. Insert a symbol.
    - On the **Insert** tab, in the **Symbols** group, click the **Symbol** drop-down arrow, and from the displayed gallery, select a symbol or;
    - Insert the symbol by using the **Symbol** dialog box.
        a. On the **Insert** tab, in the **Symbols** group, click the **Symbol** drop-down arrow, and from the displayed gallery, select **More Symbols** to display the **Symbol** dialog box.
        b. In the **Symbol** dialog box, on the **Symbols** tab, from the **Font** drop-down list, select a font that includes the symbol you want to use.
        c. In the Symbol gallery, select a symbol and click **Insert** or double-click a symbol to directly insert it.
        d. Click **Close** to close the **Symbol** dialog box.
3. Insert a special character.
    a. Open the **Symbol** dialog box and select the **Special Characters** tab.
    b. Select the desired special character and click **Insert** or double-click the special character to insert it and click **Close.**.

The Wingdings Font

Wingdings is a font available in Word that includes many decorative symbols. Wingding symbols represents some common computer components and other elements of graphical user interfaces.

ACTIVITY 4-1
Inserting Symbols and Special Characters

Data Files:

C:\084582Data\Inserting Special Characters and Graphical Objects\OGC Properties.docx

Scenario:

You have finished drafting the OGC Properties document. In the Legal Information section, the company style guide requires a registered trademark character to follow the "Rates of Interest" publication name, and a copyright character between the word "copyright" and the year in which the document was published. In addition to this, the style guide requires that the word "Phone" in the "Contact Information" text be replaced by a Wingdings telephone symbol.

1. Insert the registered trademark special character.

   a. On the Quick Access toolbar, click the **Open.** button.

   b. From theC:\084582Data\Inserting Special Characters and Graphical Objects folder, open the OGC Properties.docx file.

   c. Scroll down to display the Rates of Interest section on the fifth page and in the Legal Information paragraph place the insertion point after the italicized text "Rates of Interest."

   d. Select the **Insert** tab, and in the **Symbols** group, click the **Symbol** drop-down arrow Ω Symbol, and from the displayed gallery, select the **Registered sign (®)** symbol.

2. Insert the copyright symbol.

   a. In the same paragraph, place the insertion point after the text "copyright."

   b. On the **Insert** tab, in the **Symbols** group, click the **Symbol** drop-down arrow, and from the displayed gallery, select the **Copyright sign (©)** symbol.

   € £ ¥ © ®
   ™ ± ≠ ≤ ≥
   ÷ × ∞ µ ɑ
   β ∏ Ω ∑ ☺
   Ω More Symbols...

3. Replace the word "Phone" with the Wingdings telephone symbol.

   a. Below the "Contact Information" subheading, select the word "Phone."

   b. On the **Insert** tab, in the **Symbols** group, click the **Symbol** drop-down arrow, and from the displayed gallery select **More Symbols.**

c. In the **Symbol** dialog box, on the **Symbols** tab, in the **Font** drop-down list, scroll down and select **Wingdings.**

d. In the Symbol gallery, select the telephone symbol ☎.

e. Click **Insert** and click **Close.**

f. Save the document as *My OGC Properties* in the DOCX format.

TOPIC B

Add Illustrations to a Document

You inserted text symbols and special characters to add clarity to documents. You need not restrict yourself to just symbols and graphics because Word comes with features to add other colorful visual elements to a document too. In this topic, you will enhance documents by adding illustrations to them.

You have formatted text to the extent you can without it becoming a distraction, yet the document needs something to make it visually appealing. You may want to insert a simple image in the document to support the message in the text. With the use of relevant graphics, you will be able to draw the attention of the readers to the information that you want to emphasize. In addition to features for inserting images in a document, Word provides an extensive catalog of professionally-created pictures that you can add to the documents to make them eye catching.

Illustrations

Definition:

Illustrations are graphics or media elements that you can insert in documents to provide visual representations of text, or to add visual interest to documents. Illustrations can include geometric shapes, pictures, or charts. After you insert illustrations, you can resize them, move them, and adjust how they should be displayed in the document.

Example:

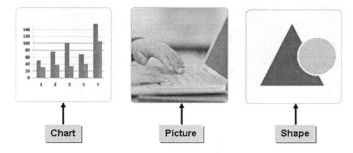

Figure 4-3: Types of illustrations that can be used in Word documents.

SmartArt

SmartArt graphics are graphic elements that combine text, illustrations, and color. They can be used to show a timeline or developmental progression. SmartArt graphics can also represent the sequential steps in a process or workflow. They are highly customizable to suit your exact information needs.

Charts

A chart is a graphical representation of statistical data. Charts are used to visually represent a relationship between different groups of data. There are different types of charts such as Bar, Pie, and Line.

Clip Art

Definition:

A *clip art* image is a type of illustration that generally is not a photograph, and has a simple two-dimensional appearance. Clip art are used to illustrate ideas in a variety of documents in electronic and print format. Unlike photographs, clip art are simple graphics composed of lines, curves, shapes, and color fills. A number of default clip art are available for use in documents created in software applications such as Word.

Example:

Figure 4-4: *A clip art illustration.*

Pictures

Definition:

A *picture* is a type of illustration that closely resembles a real object. In Word, pictures can be digital renderings of paintings, digital photographs, or computer graphics. They are stored in files that use a graphic format such as JPEG, GIF, or BMP. Pictures can be of any size or shape.

 When you insert images in a Word document the images are embedded in the document causing the size of the document to increase. Documents with large images or many images might be of large size resulting in them being difficult to email or download.

Example:

Illustrations closely resembling a real object

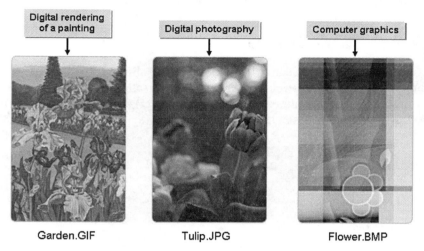

Garden.GIF   Tulip.JPG   Flower.BMP

Figure 4-5: Types of pictures that can be used in Word documents.

Microsoft Clip Organizer

Microsoft Clip Organizer is an application which is used to organize clips such as clip art, pictures, and media clips. Installed as a part of the Microsoft Office suite, you can use the clip organizer to search for clips available in your system, or from the Microsoft Office website. Clips can be organized in collections for easy retrieval. By default, clips are organized into two collections: **Office Collections** and **Web Collections**. The **Office Collections** stores all clip art available on the system as part of the Microsoft Office installation. The **Web Collections** stores clips from the Microsoft Office website.

Figure 4-6: The Microsoft Clip Organizer displaying in the category.

Within each collection, clips are organized in folders representing their relevant category. You can also create custom collections and copy clips to them. In addition, you can view the properties of clips and assign or edit keywords associated with each clip.

The Clip Art Task Pane

The **Clip Art** task pane is used to search for media files or clips of various types that are stored on a computer and from the web. You can search for clip art, photographs, movies, and sound files by entering a word or phrase that describes the clip you want to find. You can also use the **Clip Art** task pane to access **Office Online** to download additional clips.

Figure 4-7: *Clip art displayed in the Clip Art task pane.*

Clip Properties

To view a clip's properties, such as its file name, file size, creation date, search keywords associated with it, or to preview a clip, move the mouse pointer over the clip's thumbnail image and click the drop-down arrow to display the menu. Choose **Preview/Properties** to open the **Preview/Properties** dialog box, where you can preview the clip art and view its properties.

Contextual Tabs

Contextual tabs are additional tabs displayed on the Ribbon when you work with objects such as tables, pictures, or shapes. The commands and options available on these tabs are restricted to those that can be used to manipulate the objects associated with the respective tab. Contextual tabs are displayed along with the core Ribbon tabs and can be used to modify and format the objects that are displayed. You can switch between the contextual tabs and the core tabs as needed.

Figure 4-8: *The Drawing Tools contextual tab displaying options to format an object.*

Picture Tools Format Contextual Tab

The groups on the **Picture Tools Format** contextual tab can be used to control the display of illustrations in a document.

Figure 4-9: *The Picture Tools Format contextual tab displaying options to format pictures.*

Group	Allows You To
Adjust	Format images by increasing or decreasing the color, brightness, or contrast.
Picture Styles	Select a style, shape, border, and effect for a picture.
Arrange	Position an image in the document. By using the options in this group, you can also rotate, group, or align the pictures within a page.
Size	Crop an image and increase or decrease its height and width.

How to Add Illustrations to a Document

Procedure Reference: Insert a Clip Art

To insert a clip art:

1. Position the insertion point where you want to insert a clip art.
2. On the **Insert** tab, in the **Illustrations** group, click **Clip Art.**
3. In the **Clip Art** task pane, in the **Search for** text box, type a word or phrase that describes the clip art you want to locate.
4. If necessary, narrow down the search.
   - From the **Results Should Be** drop-down list, select the types of media files you want to find.
   - Check the **Include Office.com content** check box to search for clips from Office.com.
5. Click **Go** to begin the search.
6. In the section where clips are displayed, click a clip to insert it where the insertion point is placed.
7. If necessary, drag the sizing handles to adjust the clip's size.

Procedure Reference: Insert a Picture from a File

To insert a picture from a file:

1. Position the insertion point where you want to insert a picture.
2. On the **Insert** tab, in the **Illustrations** group, click **Picture.**
3. In the **Insert Picture** dialog box, navigate to the folder where the picture you want to insert is stored.
4. Select the picture and click **Insert** to insert the picture in the document.
5. If necessary, drag the sizing handles to adjust the size of the picture.

Procedure Reference: Group and Ungroup Clip Art

To group and ungroup clip art:

1. Insert a clip art or select a clip art that is inserted in a document.
2. On the **Picture Tools Format** contextual tab, in the **Arrange** group, from the **Group** drop-down list, select **Ungroup.**
3. If necessary, move or resize an ungrouped object of the clip art.
   - Move the mouse pointer over the clip art, and when the pointer turns into a cross-hair pointer, click and drag the object to move it.
   - Select an ungrouped object of the clip art, and click and drag a sizing handle to resize the object.
4. If necessary, select all the ungrouped objects in the clip art and on the **Picure Tools Format** tab, in the **Arrange** group, from the **Group** drop-down list, select **Group.**

Procedure Reference: Organize Clip Art

To organize clip art:

1. Choose **Start→All Programs→Microsoft Office→Microsoft Office Tools 2010→ Microsoft Clip Organizer.**

2. Open the **Search** task pane.

   ● From the **View** menu, choose **Search** or;

   ● On the standard toolbar, click **Search.**

3. Search for clip art.

   ● In the **Search** task pane, in the **Search for** text box, type the keyword you want to base the search on.

 If no keywords are typed in the **Search for** text box, the search returns all the clip art which satisfy the other criteria.

   ● If necessary, from the **Results should be** drop-down list, select the desired media file types to include in the search results.

   ● If necessary, check the **Include Office.com content** check box to search for clip art available on the Microsoft Office website.

   ● Click **Go** to display the clip art that satisfy the search criteria.

4. If necessary, display the **Collection List** task pane.

   ● From the **View** menu, choose **Collection List** or;

   ● On the standard toolbar, click **Collection List.**

5. If necessary, create a collection.

   a. In the **Collection List** task pane, select the **My Collections** folder.

   b. Display the **New Collection** dialog box.

      ■ From the **File** menu, choose **New Collection** or;

      ■ Right-click the **My Collections** folder and choose **New Collection.**

   c. In the **New Collection** dialog box, in the **Name** text box, type a name for the collection.

   d. If necessary, in the **Select where to place the collection** list box, select a folder in which the collection is to be created.

   e. Click **OK.**

6. Copying a clip art to a collection.

   ● Select a clip art, click the drop-down arrow, and select **Copy to Collection**. In the **Copy to Collection** dialog box, select the relevant folder and click **OK** or;

   ● Select a clip art and from the **Edit** menu, choose **Copy to Collection**. In the **Copy to Collection** dialog box, select the relevant folder and click **OK.**

7. If necessary, copy a clip art to a Word document.

   a. Copy a clip art.

      ■ Select a clip art, click the drop-down arrow, and select **Copy.**

      ■ Select a clip art, and from the **Edit** menu, choose **Copy.**

   b. Switch to the Word document.

   c. Place the insertion point in the desired location.

   d. Paste the clip art.

ACTIVITY 4-2
Adding Clip Art to a document

Data Files:

C:\084582Data\Inserting Special Characters and Graphical Objects\OGC Properties.docx

Before You Begin
The My OGC Properties.docx file is open.

Scenario:
Because the Rates of Interest section in the OGC Properties document is going to be a monetary guide that will be frequently used by your coworkers and their clients, you want the section to be instantly identifiable. To help accomplish this, you decide to add a company logo and a simple image that depicts money.

1. Search for clip art that are related to money.

    a. On the **Insert** tab, in the **Illustrations** group, click **Clip Art** to display the **Clip Art** task pane.

    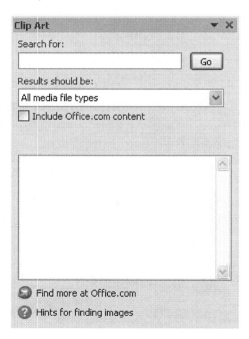

    b. In the **Clip Art** task pane, in the **Search for** text box, click and type *money*

c. Click the **Results should be** drop-down arrow, and in the displayed options, uncheck the **Photographs, Videos,** and **Audio** check boxes to limit the search to clip art.

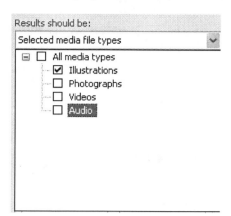

d. Click **Go** to display all the clip art that are related to money.

2. Insert the orange dollar ($) symbol clip art.

a. In the document, position the insertion point at the end of the heading "Rates of interest."

b. Select the orange clip art which displays the dollar ($) symbol to insert it into the document.

c. In the **Clip Art** task pane, at the top right corner, click the **Close** button.

3. Insert the OGC Properties logo.

a. Place the insertion point at the beginning of the heading "Rates of Interest" and press **Enter.**

b. Press the **Up Arrow** key to move the insertion point to the previous line, and select the **Insert** tab, and in the **Illustrations** group, click **Picture.**

c. In the **Insert Picture** dialog box, navigate to the C:\084582Data\Inserting Special Characters and Graphical Objects folder.

d. Select **OGC Logo.png** and click **Insert.**

e. Click at the end of the heading "Rates of Interest" to deselect the image.

f. Save and close the document.

Lesson 4 Follow-up

In this lesson, you inserted special characters and graphical objects into a Word document. With these enhancements, you will not only be able to add visual appeal to the Word document that you create but also increase the interest of the readers.

1. **Which symbols and special characters will you use often during the course of your work?**

2. **What is your opinion about the use of images in Word documents? How do you intend to use them in your documents?**

5 | Organizing Data in Tables

Lesson Time: 1 hour(s), 15 minutes

Lesson Objectives:

In this lesson, you will organize data in tables.

You will:

- Insert a table.
- Modify the structure of a table.
- Format a table using contextual tabs.
- Convert text to a table.

Introduction

You inserted special characters and graphical objects to make a document visually appealing. You can also present text in a structured form to improve readability and comprehension. In this lesson, you will organize data in tables.

Some types of content and numerical data can be difficult to comprehend when presented as a list or paragraph. Tables, when appropriately used, can significantly improve a reader's comprehension by allowing you to better organize and present the required information.

TOPIC A

Insert a Table

You added illustrations to a Word document to make it visually appealing. You can also present text in an appealing manner by structuring it in a form that makes it easy to read. In this topic, you will insert tables in a document.

Effective documents need to present all types of information in a way that is most comprehensible to the reader. In a document that contains text and numerical data, if the numerical data is buried along with the textual information, it becomes difficult to read and comprehend. Arranging such data in a table usually benefits the reader and makes information more accessible.

Tables

Definition:

A *table* is a grid-style container that is used to organize text, data, or pictures. Tables consist of boxes called cells that are arranged in vertical columns and horizontal rows. Each cell stores a piece of information. A table can have specialized table formats such as borders drawn around some or all of the cells.

Example:

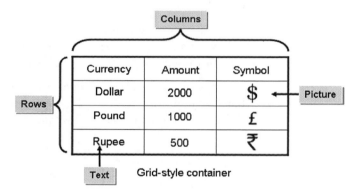

Figure 5-1: Table containing data in rows and columns.

Table Creation Options

To create a table, you can select an option from the **Table** drop-down list, in the **Tables** group, on the **Insert** tab.

Option	Description
Table grids	Allows you to move the mouse pointer over a grid and insert a table with the desired number of rows and columns. This option automatically defines the column delimiters.
Insert Table	Displays the **Insert Table** dialog box with options to create a table.

Option	Description
Draw Table	Enables you to manually draw a table.
Quick Tables	Allows you to select a predefined table from the Quick Tables gallery.
Excel Spreadsheet	Allows you to insert an Excel spreadsheet as a table. When you select the inserted table, Word provides you with all the features and tools available in Excel as options on the Ribbon.

Quick Tables

Quick tables are predefined tables that have a style applied to them and contain sample data entered in the cells. You can use the Quick Tables gallery to quickly insert a new table with a predefined format rather than having a plain grid of cells. You can then edit the placeholder text in the table to suit your needs. In Word, the Quick Tables gallery can be accessed from the **Tables** group on the **Insert** tab. There are different types of Quick Tables, such as calendars, double tables, and tables with subheadings. Quick Tables may apply a coordinated set of different fonts and column *delimiters* to a table.

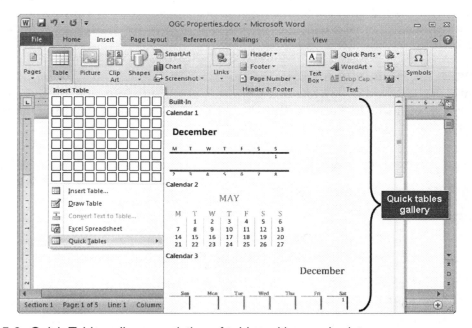

Figure 5-2: *Quick Table gallery consisting of tables with sample data.*

Table Navigation Methods

Although you can click a table cell to select it and enter text, it is more efficient to use keyboard techniques to navigate within a table.

Action	Press This Key
Move one cell to the right	**Tab** or **Right Arrow**
Move one cell to the left	**Shift+Tab** or **Left Arrow**
Move down one row	**Down Arrow**
Move up one row	**Up Arrow**

Non-Printing Characters in Tables

There are several non-printing characters that are specific to tables in Word. Each cell contains an end-of-cell marker to indicate the end of that cell. To the right of each row is an end-of-row marker that indicates the end of that row. A column marker is displayed in the ruler, at the boundary of each column. You can use these markers to select table elements. In addition to these markers, Word also displays non-printing gridlines around the table cells. Gridlines are sometimes called boundaries. If a table has borders applied to it, the gridlines will be displayed beneath the borders.

Add a Row to the Bottom of a Table

When you use the keyboard to navigate in a table, it is possible to inadvertently add a new row to the bottom of the table. Pressing **Tab** when the insertion point is located in the last cell will add a new row. If you do not want the extra row, you can undo the action.

How to Insert a Table

Procedure Reference: Create a Table

To create a table:

1. Place the insertion point where you want to insert the table.
2. On the **Insert** tab, in the **Tables** group, click the **Table** drop-down arrow.
3. From the displayed gallery, select an option to insert a table.
   - Insert the table by using the grid.
     a. Move the mouse pointer over the grid to select the desired number of rows and columns that need to be displayed in the table.

 Each cell in the grid represents one cell in the table.

     b. Click the desired cell to insert a table with the specified number of rows and columns.
   - Insert the table by using the **Insert Table** dialog box.
     a. Select **Insert Table** to display the **Insert Table** dialog box.

b. In the **Insert Table** dialog box, in the **Number of columns** and **Number of rows** spin boxes, set the desired number of columns and rows respectively, and click **OK** to insert the table.

- Insert the table by using the **Draw Table** option or;

a. Select **Draw Table.**

b. Click the pencil-shaped mouse pointer at the desired location to position the top-left corner of the table, and drag to the desired location of the bottom-right corner of the table to draw the table border.

c. Click and drag from the top border to the bottom border to define a column for the table. If necessary, draw more columns.

d. Click and drag from the left border to the right border to define a row for the table. If necessary, draw more rows.

e. Press **Esc** to deselect the pencil tool.

- Insert a table with Excel data.

a. Select **Excel Spreadsheet** to insert a blank Excel spreadsheet in the document.

b. Enter the required data in the Excel spreadsheet, or copy data from an Excel worksheet and paste it in the blank spreadsheet.

c. Click outside the spreadsheet to convert it into a table.

4. In the table, enter the table data.

Procedure Reference: Insert a Quick Table

To insert a quick table:

1. Place the insertion point where you want to insert the quick table.
2. On the Insert tab, in the Tables group, click the Tables drop-down arrow and from the displayed gallery, select Quick Tables.
3. From the gallery of predefined tables, select the table of your choice.
4. In the inserted table, replace the sample data with your own data.

Add a Tab Character to a Cell

You cannot use **Tab** on the keyboard to insert a tab character in a table because pressing **Tab** will move the insertion point to the next cell. To insert a tab within a cell, press **Ctrl+Tab.**

Type Text Before a Table

When a table is at the beginning of a document, there is no obvious way to type text above the table. The trick is to place the insertion point in the first cell of the first row of the blank table and press **Enter.** This inserts a paragraph mark above the table. You can then type the required text.

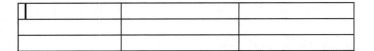

OGC Properties, Inc.
We'll find the right property for you!

Figure 5-3: *Insertion point in the first cell of the table to enable typing text above the table.*

Use Tables to Control Page Layouts

Tables are used to organize both text as well as graphics and enable you to control the page layouts. Though tables can be used to create various page layouts, they are primarily used in web page designing as they have control over the text and the graphics in a page. Arranging content in columns, applying different backgrounds and colors for different areas of a page, adjusting the size and width of different text areas can be achieved by using tables. This flexibility with tables helps provide control over page layouts to a greater extent.

ACTIVITY 5-1
Inserting a Table

Data Files:

OGC Properties.docx, New Associates and Mortgage Rates.docx

Scenario:

Your manager has provided you with a document named New Associates and Mortgage Rates that contains the content that he wants you to add in the OGC Properties document. The details of new associates and mortgage loan rates present in the document are rather difficult to read in the paragraph form. You decide that the data for new associates will read better in the form of a table, with a row for each salesperson and a column for each of the other pieces of data. You also prefer to enter the details of mortgage rates in another table.

Location	Rate%
Los Angeles, CA	6.73
Denver, CO	6.82
Washington, DC	6.63
Miami, FL	6.79
Atlanta, GA	6.75

1. Insert a table by using the **Insert Table** dialog box.

   a. On the Quick Access toolbar, click the **Open** button.

   b. In the **Open** dialog box, navigate to the C:\084582Data\Organizing Data in Tables folder.

   c. Select **OGC Properties.docx** and click **Open.**

   d. Scroll down to page four, place the insertion point after the heading "New Sales Associates," and press **Enter.**

    You can also scroll up and down a document using the **Page Up** and **Page Down** keys on the keyboard.

e. Select the **Insert** tab, and in the **Tables** group, click the **Table** drop-down arrow, and from the displayed gallery, select **Insert Table.**

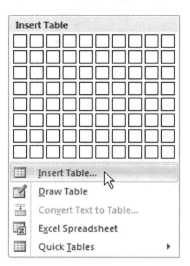

f. In the **Insert Table** dialog box, in the **Number of columns** text box, type *3* and press **Tab.**

g. In the **Number of rows** text box, type *4* and click **OK** to close the **Insert Table** dialog box and to create the table.

2. Enter data in the header row.

a. In the table, verify that the insertion point is in the first cell, type ***Associate*** and then press **Tab.**

b. Type ***Supervisor*** and press **Tab.**

c. Type ***Territory***

3. Edit the heading.

a. Press **Shift+Tab** twice to navigate to the cell with the text "Associate."

b. Type ***New Associate*** to replace the old heading with the new one.

4. Enter the new sales associates data.

a. Press the **Down Arrow** key to move the insertion point to the first cell in the second row.

b. Type ***Tim Jones*** and press **Tab.**

c. Type ***Kris Rogers*** as the supervisor and press **Tab.**

d. Type ***Los Angeles*** as the territory and press **Tab.**

e. Similarly, enter the data for Missy Lu and Miles Rodriguez by referring to the details in New Associates and Mortgage Rates.docx in the C:\084582Data\Organizing Data in Tables folder.

5. Insert a quick table.

a. Scroll down to the fifth page and click the blank line after the heading "30-year fixed-rate mortgage loan rates."

b. Select the **Insert** tab, and in the **Tables** group, click the **Table** drop-down arrow, and from the displayed gallery, select **Quick Tables.**

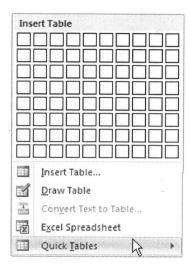

c. In the Quick Tables gallery, scroll down and select **Tabular List.**

d. In the table, double-click the word "ITEM," type *Location* and press **Tab.**

e. Type *Rate%* and press **Tab.**

f. In the second row, type *Los Angeles, CA* and press **Tab.**

g. Type *6.73* and press **Tab.**

h. Similarly, fill the cells with the data given in the New Associates and Mortgage Rates.docx document from the C:\084582Data\Organizing Data in Tables folder.

i. Save the document as *My OGC Properties* in the DOCX format.

j. Close the New Associates and Mortgage Rates.docx document.

TOPIC B
Modify a Table

You added a table to a document. As you work with the table, you may find that it contains more rows or columns than required, or that the size of some cells needs to be adjusted. In this topic, you will modify the structure of a table in a Word document.

Imagine you have created a table for the third-quarter report that shows the year-to-date revenues for your territory. Then, your manager decides it would be best to include a full year's worth of data and compare it to the same data for another territory. You will need extra columns and rows and you might even need to move some of the existing information around. You could start from scratch and create a whole new table structure, but then you would have to re-enter all existing information. Instead, you could modify the structure of the existing table to meet the new requirements.

The Table Tools Layout Contextual Tab

The **Table Tools Layout** contextual tab contains groups with options to modify the layout of a table.

Figure 5-4: The Table Tools Layout Contextual tab with options to modify the table layout.

Group	Provides Options To
Table	Select a table or the cells of a table, show or hide gridlines, and display the properties of a table.
Rows & Columns	Modify a table structure by inserting or deleting rows or columns.
Merge	Merge or split tables and cells.
Cell Size	Change the height of rows and width of columns in a table. You can also distribute the selected rows and the selected columns with equal height and equal width respectively.
Alignment	Modify the alignment of the text in a table and change the direction in which the text is entered. You can also change the default value of each cell's margins.
Data	Sort, calculate, or convert the information in a table into text. You can also use this group to repeat the header rows on every page when a table extends beyond a single page.

The Table Properties Dialog Box

The **Table Properties** dialog box allows you to specify the settings for rows, columns, individual cells, or an entire table. The options are provided on different tabs in the dialog box.

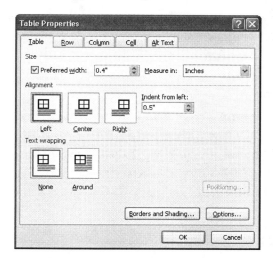

Figure 5-5: *The Table Properties dialog box displaying tabs with options to modify the table settings.*

Tab	Contains Options To
Table	Set the size, alignment, and text wrapping of a table.
Row	Set the height of the selected row. This tab also allows you to apply a page break and navigate to the previous or next row.
Column	Modify the size of the selected column. This tab also allows you to navigate to the previous or next column.
Cell	Modify the size and vertical alignment of text in the selected cell.
Alt Text	Enter alternative text information. This information is displayed when a table is displayed by using a web browser.

How to Modify a Table

Procedure Reference: Insert Rows or Columns

To insert rows or columns:

1. Position the insertion point adjacent to the column or row where you want to insert columns or rows. To insert multiple columns or rows, select an equivalent number of existing columns or rows from the table.
2. Select the **Table Tools Layout** contextual tab.
3. Insert the columns or rows.
   - In the **Rows & Columns** group, click **Insert Left** or **Insert Right** to insert a column to the left or right of the selected column.
   - In the **Rows & Columns** group, click **Insert Above** or **Insert Below** to insert a row above or below the selected row respectively.
   - Select the last cell of the table and press **Tab** to insert a row at the bottom of the table.

Table Selection Methods

There are many selection techniques that you can use to select the components of a table.

To Select	Do This
A row or rows	Move the mouse pointer to the blank space at the left of the desired row and when the mouse pointer changes to a right-tilted white arrow, click to select the row. You can also select several rows by clicking and dragging the mouse pointer up to the required number of rows.
A column or columns	Move the mouse pointer to the top or bottom border of the column until the mouse pointer changes to a down-headed arrow, and then click to select the column. You can also select several columns by clicking and dragging the mouse pointer up to the required number of columns.
A cell or cells	Move the mouse pointer to the blank space before the text in a cell and when the mouse pointer changes to a right-tilted dark arrow, click to select the cell. To select a group of cells, drag over the cells, or click a cell, hold down **Shift,** and click the last cell.
The entire table	Point to the table until the table selection box appears outside the top-left corner of the table, and then click the box. Or, on the **Layout** tab in the **Table** group, from the **Select** drop-down list, select **Select Table.**

Procedure Reference: Delete Rows or Columns

To delete rows or columns:

1. Position the insertion point in the desired column or row. To delete multiple rows or columns, select them as a group.

2. Delete the columns or rows.

- On the **Table Tools Layout** contextual tab, in the **Rows & Columns** group, from the **Delete** drop-down list, select **Delete Columns** or **Delete Rows** or;
- Right-click the table and choose **Delete Cells.** In the **Delete Cells** dialog box, select the **Delete entire column** or **Delete entire row** option and click **OK.**

Inserting or Deleting Cells

You can insert individual cells by selecting the **Table Tools Layout** contextual tab and clicking the **Table Insert Cells** dialog box launcher in the **Rows & Columns** group to display the **Insert Cells** dialog box. This dialog box has options to insert individual cells or entire rows or columns. You can also right-click a cell in the table and choose **Insert→Insert Cells.** You have the option to shift the existing cells down in the current columns or to the right in the current rows.

You can delete individual cells by clicking the **Delete** drop-down arrow, in the **Rows & Columns** group, on the **Table Tools Layout** contextual tab and selecting **Delete Cells.** You have the option to shift the existing cells up in the current columns or to the left in the current rows.

Procedure Reference: Move Columns or Rows

To move columns or rows:

1. Select the columns or rows that need to be moved.
2. On the **Home** tab, in the **Clipboard** group, click the **Cut** button or right-click the selection and choose **Cut.**
3. Place the insertion point where you want to paste the rows or columns.
4. On the **Home** tab, in the **Clipboard** group, click the **Paste** button or right-click in the desired row or column and in the displayed menu, in the **Paste Options** section, select a paste option.

Moving Cells

You cannot move individual cells by cutting and pasting. Instead, when you paste cells, Word replaces the content of the target cells.

Procedure Reference: Set the Column Width or Row Height

To set the column width or row height:

1. Place the insertion point in a specific row or column, or select multiple rows or columns.
2. On the **Table Tools Layout** contextual tab, in the **Table** group, click **Properties.**
3. In the **Table Properties** dialog box, set a specific column width.
   a. Select the **Column** tab.
   b. In the **Size** section, check the **Preferred width** check box.
   c. In the **Preferred width** spin box, specify the desired column width by using the up and down arrows or typing a value.
   d. If necessary, click the **Previous Column** or **Next Column** button to change the width of the previous or next column.
4. To set a specific row height, select the **Row** tab and follow a similar procedure.
5. Click **OK** to close the **Table Properties** dialog box.

6. If necessary, drag the row or column border to set an approximate row height or column width.

7. If necessary, double-click the right column boundary or the top row boundary to fit the row height or column width to the height or width of the cell content.

Procedure Reference: View Gridlines

To view gridlines:

1. Place the mouse pointer anywhere in the table.

2. On the Table Tools Layout contextual tab, in the Table group, click View Gridlines to toggle between viewing or hiding gridlines.

Procedure Reference: Split a Row or Column

To split a row or column:

1. Select the row or column that you want to split.

2. On the Table Tools Layout contextual tab, in the Merge group, click Split Cells.

3. In the **Split Cells** dialog box, specify the appropriate number of columns and rows to be split and click OK.

 You can also split individual cells in a table into rows and columns.

Procedure Reference: Merge Rows or Columns

To merge rows or columns:

1. Select the rows or columns that you want to merge.

2. On the Table Tools Layout contextual tab, in the Merge group, click Merge Cells to merge the cells in the row or column.

 You can also merge two or more cells that are placed adjacent in a row or column.

ACTIVITY 5-2
Modifying a Table

Before You Begin:

The My OGC Properties.docx file is open.

Scenario:

As you are including information about the new sales associates and their performances, your supervisor calls and reminds you about the new recruit for Massachusetts. He wants you to include this information in the document. You also realize that the columns of the table look too large; therefore, you decide to modify the column widths within the table. As you look through the other table with mortgage rates, you find that there are some unwanted rows of data in it and want to remove them from the table.

1. Insert an additional row in the table.

   a. Scroll up to the fourth page to view the "New Sales Associates" table.

   b. In the table, click at the beginning of the cell that contains the text "Miles Rodriguez."

   c. On the Ribbon, select the **Table Tools Layout** contextual tab.

   d. On the **Table Tools Layout** contextual tab, in the **Rows & Columns** group, click **Insert Below.**

2. Enter data in the new row.

   a. In the new row, in the first cell, click and type ***Bill Connor*** and press **Tab.**

   b. In the second cell, type ***Ted James*** and press **Tab.**

   c. In the last cell, type ***Massachusetts***

3. Reverse the order of the second and third columns.

a. In the table, move the mouse pointer above the top border of the "Territory" column, and when the mouse pointer changes to a down-headed arrow, click to select the column.

The Sales Column

New Sales Associates

New Associate	Supervisor	Territory
Tim Jones	Kris Roger	Los Angeles
Missy Lu	Chris Burke	Seattle
Miles Rodriguez	Cindy Bradley	Boston
Bill Connor	Massachusetts	Ted James

b. Select the **Home** tab, and in the **Clipboard** group, click the **Cut** button.

c. Verify that the insertion point is in the "Supervisor" column heading.

d. On the **Home** tab, in the **Clipboard** group, click **Paste.**

e. Click before the text "Territory" to deselect that column.

4. Adjust the column width to fit the content.

a. In the table, position the mouse pointer over the right border of the "New Associate" column and when the mouse pointer changes to a double-headed arrow, double-click the border to adjust the width of the column to fit its content.

b. Double-click the border to the left of the "New Associate" column to adjust the width of all the columns in the table.

5. Delete unwanted data in the mortgage rates table.

a. Scroll down to the fifth page to view the "30-year fixed-rate mortgage loan rates" table.

b. Place the mouse pointer near the left border of the cell with the text "Pencils" and when the mouse pointer changes to a right-pointing arrow, click to select the row.

c. Hold down **Shift** and click the cell with the text "1 Pair" to select the remaining rows.

d. Select the **Table Tools Layout** contextual tab, and in the **Rows & Columns** group, from the **Delete** drop-down list, select **Delete Rows** to delete the selected rows.

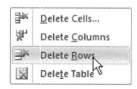

e. Save the document.

ACTIVITY 5-3
Reviewing the Modification of Table Structures

Scenario:

In this activity, you will review your knowledge of modification of table structures.

1. **Which group on the Table Tools Layout contextual tab includes the option to repeat the header rows?**

    a) The Data group

    b) The Rows & Columns group

    c) The Merge group

    d) The Table group

2. **True or False? The Row tab in the Table Properties dialog box has options to set the text wrapping of a table.**

    __ True

    __ False

TOPIC C
Format a Table

You modified the structure of a table in a Word document. You may also need to format the table to bring out the characteristics of the data in the table and improve its appearance. In this topic, you will format a table.

Although a simple table can help you present information logically, inserting a plain table in an otherwise formatted document may result in the table not being able to match the overall look of the document. Formatting a table can make the information stand out and draw the reader's attention to the table's content. Word provides various preformatted table designs that you can choose from and apply to a table so that it looks well formatted and blends with the other content in the Word document.

Table Styles

Definition:

A *table style* is a formatting option that contains a group of table-specific formatting options packaged together to apply design and formatting changes to an existing table, all at the same time. Table styles contain formatting options that include borders, shading, colors, cell alignment, table fonts, and separate formats for the first column or row. There are various table styles from which you can select a desired style for a table. You can also modify an existing style or build a new style and add it to the gallery.

Example:

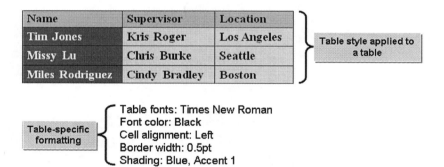

Figure 5-6: Table style applied to a table.

 To format an existing table, use a table style. To insert a preformatted table, use a Quick Table.

The Table Tools Design Contextual Tab

The **Table Tools Design** contextual tab contains groups with options to format a table.

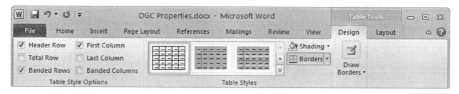

Figure 5-7: *The Table Tools Design contextual tab displaying options to modify the table format.*

Group	Enables You To
Table Style Options	Format a table by differentiating between specified rows or columns.
Table Styles	Format a table by using a set of predefined styles. It also provides options to color the background and apply borders.
Draw Borders	Draw borders on a table. It also contains options to change the line style, color, and thickness of the border. You can also erase the border.

How to Format a Table

Procedure Reference: Apply a Table Style to a Table

To apply a table style to a table:

1. Select a table.
2. On the **Table Tools Design** contextual tab, in the **Table Styles** group, click the **More** button, and from the displayed gallery, select a style to apply to the table.
3. Select a row or column.
4. Format the selected section of the table.
   - In the **Table Style Options** group, select the desired option.
     - Check the **Header Row** check box to apply special formatting for the first row.
     - Check the **Total Row** check box to apply special formatting for the last row.
     - Check the **Banded Rows** check box to apply different formatting for even number and odd number of rows.
     - Check the **First Column** check box to apply special formatting for the first column.
     - Check the **Last Column** check box to apply special formatting for the last column.

- Check the **Banded Columns** check box to apply different formatting for even number and odd number of columns.

- In the **Table Styles** group, click **Shading** and select the desired color to apply shading.

- In the **Table Styles** group, from the **Borders** drop-down list, select the desired border to apply a border.

- In the **Draw Borders** group, select the desired options to draw a border or erase the existing border.

  - From the **Line Style** drop-down list, select an option to change the line style of the borders.

  - From the **Line Width** drop-down list, select an option to change the width of borders.

  - From the **Pen Color** drop-down list, select a color to draw borders in the selected color.

  - Click **Draw Table** and in the document draw the borders for a table.

  - Click **Eraser** and in the document erase the borders of a table.

Procedure Reference: Define a Header Row

To define a header row:

1. Place the mouse pointer anywhere in the table.

2. On the Table Tools Design contextual tab, in the Table Style Options group, check the Header Row check box to enable formatting for the header row.

3. In the Table Styles group, from the Table Styles gallery, select a table style with the desired header row formatting.

4. If necessary, select the header row, and on the Table Tools Layout contextual tab, in the Data group, click Repeat Header Rows to repeat the header row on all the pages where the table gets extended.

 You can select the first row along with the subsequent rows and repeat them as header rows on the pages where the table is extended.

ACTIVITY 5-4
Formatting a Table

Before You Begin:

The My OGC Properties.docx file is open.

Scenario:

You have included all the details in the New Sales Associate table as per your supervisor's requirement and also removed unwanted data in the 30-year fixed rate mortgage loan rates table. Before you submit the document for your supervisor's review, you decide to format both the tables to make them visually appealing.

1. Apply a style to the "New Sales Associates" table.

   a. Scroll up to the fourth page to view the "New Sales Associates" table.

   b. Place the insertion point before the text "New Associate" in the first cell of the table.

   The Sales Column

   New Sales Associates

New Associate	Supervisor	Territory
Tim Jones	Kris Roger	Los Angeles
Missy Lu	Chris Burke	Seattle
Miles Rodriguez	Cindy Bradley	Boston
Bill Connor	Massachusetts	Ted James

   c. Select the **Table Tools Design** contextual tab, and in the **Table Styles** group, click the **More** button.

   d. In the displayed gallery, and in the **Built-In** section, select the **Table Colorful 2** style, which is the second style in the second row.

2. Apply borders to the table.

   a. Select the **Table Tools Layout** contextual tab, and in the **Table** group, from the **Select** drop-down list, select **Select Table.**

   b. Select the **Table Tools Design** contextual tab, and in the **Table Styles** group, from the **Borders** drop-down list, select **All Borders** to apply borders to the entire table.

3. Apply a style to the "30-year fixed rate mortgage loan rates" table.

   a. Scroll down to the fifth page to view the "30-year fixed rate mortgage loan rates" table.

   b. Place the insertion point in the first cell of the table.

   c. Select the **Table Tools Layout** contextual tab, and in the **Table** group, from the **Select** drop-down list, select **Select Table.**

d. Select the **Table Tools Design** contextual tab, and in the **Table Styles** group, click the **More** button

e. In the displayed gallery, in the **Built-in** section, scroll up and select the **Table List 1** style, which is the fifth style in the fourth row.

f. In the **Table Style Options** group, check the **Banded Rows** check box to apply special formatting for the rows in the table.

g. Save the document.

ACTIVITY 5-5
Examining the Table Formatting Options

Scenario:

In this activity, you will examine the table formatting options available in Word.

1. **Which group on the Table Tools Design contextual tab has options to draw borders for a table?**

   a) The Table Style Options group

   b) Draw Borders group

   c) Table group

   d) Table Styles group

2. **Which tabs have options to insert and format a table?**

   a) The Insert tab

   b) The Home tab

   c) The Table Tools Design contextual tab

   d) The Table Tools Layout contextual tab

TOPIC D

Convert Text to a Table

You created tables and entered content in them manually. When you already have information in a document, Word provides options to convert this information into a table. In this topic, you will convert existing text into a new table as well as convert content in a table back to text.

Imagine that you are updating a product catalog sheet, when you realize that the information would be more readable if it is put in a formatted table. However, because the document is several pages long, it will take a long time to retype and format all the information in a new table, not to mention the fact that you may make mistakes while typing. The most efficient way to approach this dilemma is to use the options in Word to convert the existing tabbed text into a table, without the risk of mistakes, while formatting the table simultaneously.

The Convert Text to Table Dialog Box

If you have used tab characters to create columns of data in a document, you can convert the tabbed text to a table by using the options in various sections of the **Convert Text to Table** dialog box.

Figure 5-8: *The Convert Text to Table dialog box displaying options to convert text to a table.*

Section	Description
Table size	Provides options to specify the number of rows and columns to suit the table content.
AutoFit behavior	Provides options to specify how the table columns are sized to fit the contents in the table. Columns can be of fixed width, equally sized to fit the document width, or variable sized depending on the content of each column.
Separate text at	Provides options to specify whether paragraphs, tabs, commas, or any other options should be considered as a delimiter to split the text into table cells, while converting the text into a table.

The Convert Table to Text Dialog Box

You can use the **Convert Table To Text** dialog box to convert the text in a table to paragraph format. It provides options to separate the data in the table by using paragraph marks, tabs, commas, or other delimiting characters, when it is converted into text. You can access the **Convert Table To Text** dialog box from the **Data** group on the **Table Tools Layout** contextual tab.

Figure 5-9: *The Convert Table to Text dialog box displaying options to convert a table to text.*

How to Convert Text to a Table

Procedure Reference: Convert Tabbed Text to a Table

To convert tabbed text to a table:

1. Select the text that you want to convert to a basic table.
2. On the **Insert** tab, in the **Tables** group, click the **Table** drop-down arrow, and from the displayed gallery, select **Insert Table.**

Procedure Reference: Convert Text to a Table by Using the Convert Text to Table Dialog Box

To convert text to a table by using the **Convert Text to Table** dialog box:

1. Select the text that you want to convert into a table.
2. On the **Insert** tab, in the **Tables** group, click the **Table** drop-down arrow, and from the displayed gallery, select **Convert Text to Table.**
3. In the **Convert Text to Table** dialog box, set the table properties.

    *   In the **Table size** section, specify the desired number of rows and columns by using the up and down arrows in the spin boxes or typing a number in the spin boxes.

    *   In the **AutoFit behavior** section, select the options to automatically modify the size of the rows and columns to suit the content.

    *   In the **Separate text at** section, select an option to set the delimiter character.

4. Click **OK** to insert the table.

Procedure Reference: Convert a Table to Text by Using the Convert Table To Text Dialog Box

To convert a table to text by using the **Convert Table To Text** dialog box:

1. Select the desired table.
2. On the **Table Tools Layout** contextual tab, in the **Data** group, click **Convert to Text.**
3. In the **Convert Table To Text** dialog box, select the desired option to set a delimiter character for the data, and click **OK** to convert the table to text.

ACTIVITY 5-6
Converting Text into a Table

Data Files:

Points of Interst.docx

Before You Begin:

The My OGC Properties.docx file is open.

Scenario:

Your coworker has added some content to the OGC Properties document. She has used tabs to separate the data in the document. You want to make the data more readable, without spending too much time on it. Therefore, you decide to convert the tabbed text into a table.

Your coworker has also sent you data on points of interest that has to be included in the OGC Properties document. You find that the data is in table format, and feel that it is more readable when presented in the form of a paragraph.

---

1. Convert the Junior Sales Associate Performance Review data into a basic table.

    a. Scroll up to the fourth page, and in the second paragraph under the title "Junior Sales Associate Performance Review," select the names of the Junior Associates "Tim Jones, Missy Lu, Miles Rodriguez," and "Bill Connor" along with the text associated with each name.

    b. Select the **Insert** tab, and in the **Tables** group, click the **Table** drop-down arrow, and from the displayed gallery, select **Insert Table.**

    c. Observe that the tabbed text is displayed in a table.

    d. Click away from the table to deselect it.

---

2. Convert the Junior Sales Associate Sales data into a table that exactly fits the contents.

    a. Scroll down to the top of the fifth page.

    b. Select the five lines of tabbed data "Jr. Sales Associate..." through "1".

    c. Select the **Insert** tab, and in the **Tables** group, click the **Table** drop-down arrow, and from the displayed gallery, select **Convert Text to Table.**

d. In the **Convert Text to Table** dialog box, verify that the **Number of Columns** spin box contains the value **4,** select the **AutoFit to contents** option, and click **OK** to convert the tabbed text into a formatted table.

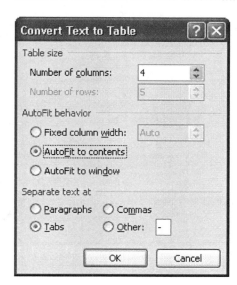

e. Click away from the table to deselect the text in the table.

3. Include content from the Points of Interest document.

   a. Navigate to the C:\084582Data\Organizing Data in Tables folder and open the Points of Interest.docx file.

   b. In the Points of Interest.docx document, on the **Home** tab, in the **Editing** group, from the **Select** drop-down list, select **Select All** to select the entire content in the document.

   c. On the **Home** tab, in the **Clipboard** group, click the **Copy** button.

   d. Close the Points of Interest document.

   e. In the My OGC Properties document, scroll down to the sixth page of the document.

   f. Place the insertion point before the title "Legal Information."

   g. On the **Home** tab, in the **Clipboard** group, click **Paste** to paste the content that you copied from the Points of Interest document.

4. Convert table to text with commas as the delimiter.

   a. Place the insertion point in the first cell of the table before the text "Mortgate Product."

   b. Select the **Table Tools Layout** contextual tab and in the **Table** group, from the **Select** drop-down list, select **Select Table.**

   c. In the **Data** group, click **Convert to Text.**

   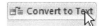

      d.   In the **Convert Table To Text** dialog box, select the **Commas** option and click **OK.**

      e.   Click anywhere in the document to deselect the text.

      f.   Save and close the document.

Lesson 5 Follow-up

In this lesson, you organized data in tables. Using tables can significantly improve readability and comprehension of data which may be difficult to read when presented as a list or paragraph.

1. **Do you expect to use tables in your document? For what reasons?**

2. **What type of information do you think you may want to include in tables?**

6 | Proofing a Word Document

Lesson Time: 45 minutes

Lesson Objectives:

In this lesson, you will proof a Word document.

You will:

- Check spelling and grammar.
- Use the thesaurus.

Introduction

You organized data in tables. Now that you have all the text content in place, you may want to check the document for errors and make the necessary corrections and updates. In this lesson, you will proof a Word document.

Finding and fixing errors in your writing goes a long way toward projecting a professional image. Proofreading, though, is a specialized, time-consuming skill. Word includes various proofing tools to simplify some of the mechanics of proofreading. These tools also help in electronically revising your documents, providing a built-in dictionary and access to other reference materials. By effectively using these proofing tools, you can ensure accuracy while you streamline the overall process of proofreading and finalizing a document.

TOPIC A

Check Spelling and Grammar

You used tables to improve the presentation of content in a document. Before finalizing the content, you may need to check the document for errors. In this topic, you will check the spelling and grammar of text in a Word document.

One of the many benefits of electronic word processing is that it makes it easy to correct all kinds of errors. It also saves you valuable time by reviewing the whole document programmatically, quickly pointing out mistakes that would take much longer to find and correct on a hard copy. Spelling, grammar, and text count tools in Word can make documents more accurate and concise.

Spelling and Grammar Check Options

Word provides you with electronic tools that enable you to check the spelling and grammar usage in a document against a built-in word list and set of grammar rules. To check the text, you can click the **Spelling & Grammar** button in the **Proofing** group on the **Review** tab. This displays the **Spelling and Grammar** dialog box which provides options to identify possible errors and suggests replacements for erroneous text.

You can also right-click a misspelled word or grammatically suspect section and choose the desired correct option from the shortcut menu. This menu can also be accessed from the status bar.

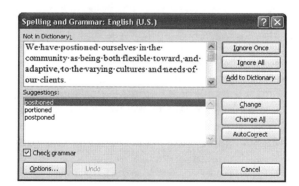

Figure 6-1: *The Spelling and Grammar dialog box displaying options to correct misspelled words.*

Options in the Spelling and Grammar Dialog Box

The **Spelling and Grammar** dialog box offers various options that help you edit the grammar usage and spelling in a document.

Option	Description
The **Not in Dictionary** text box.	Displays the words or sentences that Word identifies as errors.
The **Capitalization Error** text box.	Displays the words or sentences that has incorrect capitalization.

Option	Description
The **Fragment** text box.	Displays the sentences that convey an incomplete thought.
The **Suggestions** list box.	Displays a list of possible correct options.
The **Ignore Once** button.	Enables you to skip the occurrence of the error this time, but finds the next occurrence. In this way, you can correct errors on a case-by-case basis.
The **Ignore All** button.	Enables you to leave all instances of the highlighted text unchanged and continue searching for the next error.
The **Add to Dictionary** button.	Enables you to add the occurrence of the error to the dictionary. This will allow Word to recognize the occurrence as correct when you check spelling in the future.
The **Change** button.	Replaces the found text with the selected correction from the **Suggestions** list box.
The **Change All** button.	Replaces all occurrences of the found text with the selected correction from the **Suggestions** list box.
The **AutoCorrect** button.	Automatically replaces all instances of erroneous words or sentences.
The **Options** button.	Displays the **Proofing** tab in the **Word Options** dialog box. This tab is used to set the criteria based on which the documents are checked.
The **Undo** button.	Enables you to undo the previous edit, if you want to revert to the original text.

AutoCorrect Dialog Box

The *AutoCorrect dialog box* contains a series of tabs that you can use to control the AutoCorrect behavior.

Figure 6-2: The AutoCorrect dialog box displaying the various AutoCorrect options.

Tab	Provides Options To
AutoCorrect	Automatically edit typographical or capitalization errors.
Math AutoCorrect	Automatically replace expressions with the corresponding symbols.
AutoFormat As You Type	Automatically format the document text as you type.
AutoFormat	Automatically format the style of a document after you finish entering the contents.
Actions	Save time by allowing you to perform certain actions in Word rather than using other programs.

The Dictionary

In Word, you can use the *dictionary* to validate your spelling. When you type, or when you run the **Spelling & Grammar** command, Word compares the words to its stored dictionary list. If you have misspelled a word, or if you have used a specialized word that is not in the dictionary, the spell checker will give you a list of possible suggestions. The main dictionary is the primary dictionary used to check for errors. The main dictionary can be neither edited nor viewed. Word also has a default custom dictionary to which you can add words or names.

Custom Dictionaries

You can also create or import custom dictionaries and remove custom dictionaries when you no longer need them. To manage custom dictionaries, open the **Word Options** dialog box, select the **Proofing** tab, and then click **Custom Dictionaries.**

The Readability Statistics Dialog Box

Readability statistics are ratings that provide a measurement of the complexity level of text. If you have enabled readability statistics in Word, the *Readability Statistics dialog box* is displayed after you check the grammar usage. This dialog box provides detailed information on the total number of characters, words, sentences, and paragraphs in a document and also the average number of words per sentence, sentences per paragraph, and characters per word in the document. It also reports the readability scores for the content in the document.

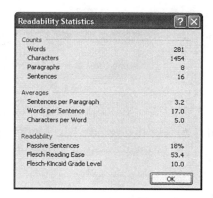

Figure 6-3: *The Readability Statistics dialog box displaying the readability information about a document.*

Grading of Readability Scores

There are different readability analysis methods. The readability scores in Word are based on the Flesch Reading Ease and the Flesch-Kincaid Grade Level scales. These scales help to evaluate the readability and complexity of the document based on the average number of syllables per word and words per sentence. Flesch Reading Ease scores text as a single number, with higher scores indicating lesser grade levels. The Flesch-Kincaid Grade Level categorizes the text according to United States public school grade-level reading standards. The two scales use slightly different formulas and have a reverse correlation; a low reading ease score correlates to a high grade level and vice versa. By using simple sentences, one can reduce the grade level. The readability scores should match the target reading audience; some government agencies require that public documents match a target readability range.

In addition, the readability statistics feature in Word tells you the percentage of sentences that use passive voice ("the ball was thrown by the boy") instead of active voice ("the boy threw the ball"). Most writing experts recommend using active voice in the majority of sentences.

The Word Count Dialog Box

Microsoft Word provides you with a running word count to ensure that a document you create fits within any content length limits. When you click **Words** on the status bar, or when you click the **Word Count** button in the **Proofing** group on the **Review** tab, the **Word Count** dialog box is displayed. This dialog box helps you keep track of the number of pages, words, characters, paragraphs, and lines in a document. As you enter text in a document, Word displays a live word count on the status bar.

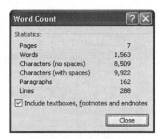

Figure 6-4: *The Word Count dialog box displaying statistics on words, characters, paragraphs, and lines in a Word document.*

The AutoCorrect Tab

The **AutoCorrect** tab in the **AutoCorrect** dialog box has a number of options that enable you to automatically edit the typographical or capitalization errors in a document.

Option	*Description*
The **Show AutoCorrect Options buttons** check box.	Displays the **AutoCorrect Options** button whenever the AutoCorrect feature edits a typographical error.
The **Correct TWo INitial CApitals** check box.	Corrects errors of entering two initial capitals for a word.
The **Capitalize first letter of sentences** check box.	Automatically capitalizes the initial letter of every sentence.
The **Capitalize first letter of table cells** check box.	Automatically capitalizes the initial letter of words entered in each cell of a table.
The **Capitalize names of days** check box.	Automatically capitalizes the initial letters of day names.
The **Correct accidental usage of cAPS LOCK key** check box.	Automatically corrects the casing of the letters in a sentence, if **Caps Lock** is accidentally activated.
The **Exceptions** button.	Allows you to make a list of words or characters that you want to retain as typed.
The **Replace text as you type** check box.	Replaces common typographical errors or other key combinations with designated words or characters. For example, as a shortcut for the words that you frequently type such as your company's name, you can enter an abbreviation that Word will expand to the full word or phrase. You should not add words that already exist in the list as shortcuts for other words. You can add words and special characters to this list, but you cannot add shapes or other graphic objects.

How to Check Spelling and Grammar

Procedure Reference: Enable Readability Statistics

To enable readability statistics:

1. Select the **File** tab and choose **Options.**

2. In the **Word Options** dialog box, select the **Proofing** tab.

3. In the **When correcting spelling and grammar in Word** section, check the **Show readability statistics** check box and click **OK.**

Procedure Reference: Set Grammar and Style Options

To set grammar and style options:

1. Select the **File** tab, and choose **Options.**

2. In the **Word Options** dialog box, select the **Proofing** tab.

3. In the **When correcting spelling and grammar in Word** section, click **Settings.**

4. In the **Grammar Settings** dialog box, from the **Writing Style** drop-down list, select the desired writing style.

   - Select **Grammar Only** to check the grammatical errors alone.
   - Select **Grammar & Style** to check grammatical as well as errors in writing style.

5. In the **Grammar and style options** section, specify the desired settings.

   - In the **Require** section, set the desired options.

     - From the **Comma required before last list item** drop-down list, select an option to specify the requirement of commas when items are listed.
     - From the **Punctuation required with quotes** drop-down list, select an option to specify the use of punctuation along with quotation marks.
     - From the **Spaces required between sentences** drop-down list, select an option to specify the need for spaces between sentences.

   - In the **Grammar** section, check the desired check boxes to set the grammar settings.
   - In the **Style** section, check the desired check boxes to set the language style settings.

6. Close the **Grammar Settings** and **Word Options** dialog boxes.

Procedure Reference: Change Grammar Checking Options

To change the grammar check options:

1. Select the **File** tab, and choose **Options.**

2. In the **Word Options** dialog box, select the **Proofing** tab.

3. In the **When correcting spelling and grammar in Word** section, check the desired options to change the grammar checking options.

4. Close the **Word Options** dialog box.

Procedure Reference: Check Spelling and Grammar Using the Contextual Menu

To check the spelling and grammar using contextual features:

1. Display the contextual menu.
   - Right-click the text with a red, wavy underline (for spelling errors) or a green, wavy underline (for grammatical errors).
   - Click the contextual spell checker button that is displayed on the status bar when Word detects a spelling or grammatical error.
2. Choose the desired correction from the context menu.

Procedure Reference: Correct Spelling and Grammar Errors

To correct spelling and grammar errors:

1. Position the insertion point at the beginning of the document to check the entire document. Alternatively, select specific text to check a selection.
2. Display the **Spelling and Grammar** dialog box.
   - On the **Review** tab, in the **Proofing** group, click **Spelling & Grammar** or;
   - Press **F7.**
3. In the **Spelling and Grammar** dialog box, correct an error.
   a. From the **Suggestions** list box, select a correct replacement for the erroneous word or phrase.
   b. Replace or ignore the error.
      - Click **Change** to replace the misspelled word with the correct selection.
      - Click **Change All** to replace all occurrences of the misspelled word with the correct selection.
      - Click **Ignore Once** to retain the word as you have entered and move on to the next error.
      - Click **Ignore All** to retain all occurrences of the word as you have entered and move on to the next error.
      - Click **Add to Dictionary** to add the misspelled word to the custom dictionary so that it does not show as an error in the future.
      - Click **AutoCorrect** to automatically replace all misspelled words and erroneous phrases with the corrections.
      - If necessary, manually edit the text in the document, and click **Resume** to move on to the next error.
4. Edit the other errors in the document as needed.
5. In the **Microsoft Word** message box, which states that Word has completed the search, click **OK.**
6. If the **Readability Statistics** dialog box is displayed, review the statistics and click **OK.**

Procedure Reference: Check the Word Count

To check the number of words in a Word document:

1. Select a section of text to count the number of words in the selection, or place the insertion point anywhere in the document to count the number of words in the entire document.

2. Display the **Word Count** dialog box.

- On the **Review** tab, in the **Proofing** group, click **Word Count** or;
- On the status bar, click the **Words** button or;
- Press **Ctrl+Shift+G.**

3. When you have finished reviewing the word count in the **Word Count** dialog box, click **Close.**

Procedure Reference: Customize the AutoCorrect Options

To customize the AutoCorrect options:

1. Display the **AutoCorrect** dialog box.

   a. Select the **File** tab and choose **Options.**

   b. In the **Word Options** dialog box, select the **Proofing** tab.

   c. In the **AutoCorrect options** section, click the **AutoCorrect Options** button.

2. In the **AutoCorrect: <language>** dialog box, check or uncheck the desired options.

3. Click **Exceptions,** and in the **AutoCorrect Exceptions** dialog box, on the appropriate tab, type the exception, and then click **OK** to add the exception.

4. If necessary, display the **AutoCorrect Exceptions** dialog box, select an exception and click **Delete** to remove the exception.

5. If necessary, add or remove more exceptions.

6. If necessary, add an abbreviation for frequently typed text.

   a. In the **Replace** section, enter an abbreviation.

   b. In the **With** section, enter the full form of the abbreviation, and then click **Add** to add the abbreviation.

7. If necessary, add more abbreviations.

8. Click **OK** to close the **AutoCorrect: <language>** dialog box.

9. Click **OK** to close the **Word Options** dialog box.

Procedure Reference: Turn On and Off AutoCorrect Options

To turn On/Off AutoCorrect:

1. Select the **File** tab, and choose **Options.**

2. In the **Word Options** dialog box, select the **Proofing** tab.

3. In the **AutoCorrect options** section, click **AutoCorrect Options.**

4. In the **AutoCorrect:<language>** dialog box, on the **AutoCorrect** tab, check the desired check boxes to enable the AutoCorrect feature.

5. If necessary, uncheck all the check boxes to turn off the AutoCorrect feature.

6. Click **OK** in the **AutoCorrect:<language>** dialog box.

ACTIVITY 6-1
Checking a Document's Spelling, Grammar, and Length

Data Files:

C:\084582Data\Proofing a Word Document\OGC Properties.docx

Scenario:

You need to make sure that you meet the deadline for completing the document on OGC Properties. You have quickly typed the necessary text because you know that you can return and correct mistakes after entering all the content. Now, you need to check for, and correct, any typographical errors. You also need to ensure that the document is not difficult to read and that the overall length of the document fits within the word limit.

1. Enable the **Readability Statistics** option.

   a. On the Quick access toolbar, click **Open.**

   b. From the C:\084582Data\Proofing a Word Document folder, open the OGC Properties.docx file.

   c. Select the **File** tab and choose **Options.**

   d. In the **Word Options** dialog box, select the **Proofing** tab.

   e. In the **When correcting spelling and grammar in Word** section, check the **Show readability statistics** check box and click **OK** to close the **Word Options** dialog box.

   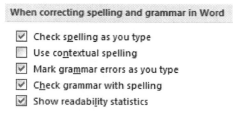

2. Correct the misspelled word and the grammar error by using the shortcut menu.

   a. Verify that the insertion point is placed at the beginning of the document.

b.   On the status bar, click the contextual spell checker button.

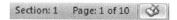

c.   Observe the statistics displayed in the **Readability Statistics** dialog box, and then click **OK** to close it.

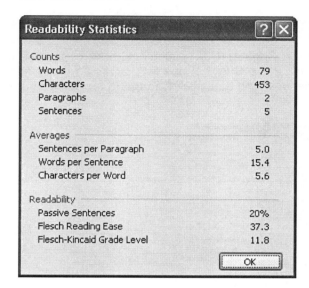

d.   Right-click the word "vrious" and from the displayed shortcut menu, choose **various** to replace the misspelled word.

e.   Scroll down and in the paragraph below the title "Our Corporate Philosophy," right-click anywhere in the text **service begin** and choose **services begin** to correct the grammar error.

3.   Make changes to the document by using the **Spelling & Grammar** command.

a. Scroll up and position the insertion point at the beginning of the document.

b. Select the **Review** tab, and in the **Proofing** group, click **Spelling & Grammar.**

c. In the **Spelling and Grammar: English (U.S.)** dialog box, observe that the word "recommendations" is selected in the **Suggestions** list box, as a replacement for the misspelled word "recomendations" and then click **Change** to replace the misspelled word.

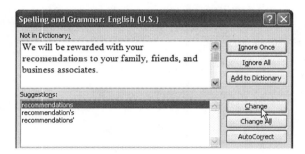

d. Observe that the word "whether" is selected in the **Suggestions** list box, and click **Change** to replace "whther" with "whether."

e. In the **Spelling and Grammar: English (U.S.)** dialog box, observe that in the **Fragment** text box, a phrase is displayed, which Word treats as an incomplete sentence. Click **Ignore Once** to ignore this occurrence of a sentence fragment.

f. In the **Microsoft Word** message box that says spelling and grammar check is complete and the text which was marked as not to be checked was skipped, click **OK.**

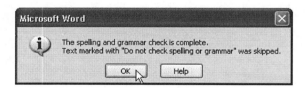

g. Review the readability statistics and click **OK** to close the **Readability Statistics** dialog box.

4. Check the number of words in the document.

a. On the status bar, right-click the contextual spell checker button, and select **Word Count.**

b. On the **Review** tab, in the **Proofing** group, click **Word Count.**

c. Observe that the document has 2887 words and 416 lines, and then click **Close.**

5. Count the words in the second paragraph.

a. Triple-click the paragraph below the heading "Description of Our Firm" to select it.

b.   On the status bar, observe that the word count is 90.

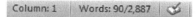

6.   Delete the last few lines of text to reduce the word count in the document.

a.   Scroll down to the bottom of page 10.

b.   Select the text from "The Tri State Area" through "San Antonio" and press **Delete.**

c.   On the **Review** tab, in the **Proofing** group, click **Word Count.**

d.   Observe that the word count and number of lines in the document has been reduced, and click **Close.**

e.   Save the document as *My OGC Properties* in the DOCX format.

ACTIVITY 6-2
Customizing the AutoCorrect Options

Before You Begin:
The My OGC Properties.docx file is open.

Scenario:
In the document that you are creating, you have multiple occurrences of the name "OGC Properties." You feel that using an abbreviation that automatically changes to this name will be helpful in saving time in the future.

1. Display the **AutoCorrect: English (U.S.)** dialog box.

   a. Select the **File** tab and choose **Options.**

   b. In the **Word Options** dialog box, select the **Proofing** tab.

   c. In the **AutoCorrect options** section, click **AutoCorrect Options.**

2. Set up data entry shortcuts for the words "OGC Properties."

   a. In the **AutoCorrect: English (U.S.)** dialog box, in the **Replace text as you type** section, in the **Replace** text box, type *op* and press **Tab** to move to the **With** text box.

   b. In the **With** text box, type *OGC Properties* and click **Add.**

   c. Click **OK** in the **AutoCorrect: English (U.S.)** and **Word Options** dialog boxes.

3. Include the necessary text in the document.

   a. Scroll up to the seventh page, and under the title "AN INVESTMENT IN CLIENT SERVICE," click at the end of the last paragraph, press the **Spacebar** and type *Our goal is for op* and then press the **Spacebar** again.

   b. Observe that "op" is replaced with "OGC Properties."

   c. Type *to have internal and affiliated offices in 150 markets within the next two years.*

   d. Save the file.

TOPIC B

Use the Thesaurus

You checked a document for spelling and grammar errors. Just as you can use the built-in spell checker in Word to fix grammatical errors, you can also use the thesaurus in Word as a substitute for another common reference, a physical thesaurus. In this topic, you will use the built-in thesaurus in Word.

Imagine that you have written a draft memo promoting the useful features of your company's new email program. When you read the draft, you find that you have described nearly every feature in the same way by using the word "useful." Using a variety of words can make a document more readable, but often it is difficult to think of different appropriate synonyms for every word. A thesaurus can be used to find alternate words, and by using the electronic thesaurus in Word, you can break the monotony of a document.

The Thesaurus

Definition:

A *thesaurus* is a reference tool that gives you a collection of synonyms and antonyms. Unlike a dictionary, a thesaurus does not provide the definition of a word. An electronic thesaurus can suggest and replace words automatically in a document. You can access the Word thesaurus from the **Proofing** group of the **Review** tab. The thesaurus is also available in various languages such as English (U.S.), French (France), and Spanish (International Sort).

Example:

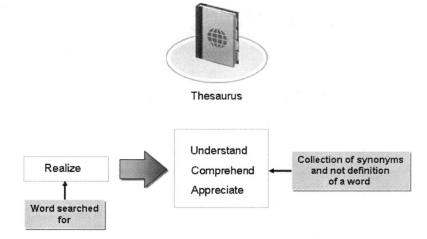

Figure 6-5: The Thesaurus displaying the collection of synonyms for a word.

The Research Task Pane

The *Research task pane* lets you look up information from a wide variety of online references, including various dictionaries and thesauruses. You can even use it to translate text from one language to another. This task pane provides access to a number of web-based research books and reference sites. To use all of the research options, you need to have an active Internet connection. You can open the **Research** task pane by clicking the **Research** button, in the **Proofing** group, on the **Review** tab.

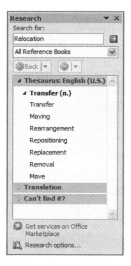

Figure 6-6: The Research task pane.

The Research Options Dialog Box

The **Research Options** dialog box allows you to customize the reference books and research sites that you want to access.

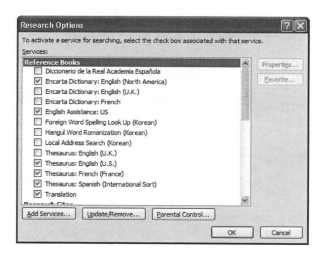

Figure 6-7: The Research Options dialog box listing the different research sevices

Option	Description
Services	Lists the various reference books and other services that you can use to search for information. You can check the desired check boxes in the **Reference Books** section.
Add Services	Opens the **Add Services** dialog box that allows you to specify the website address from where you can select services for research options. The desired service can also be selected from the **Advertised Services** list box. However, the list of advertised services is provided by Microsoft's Discovery Server. Once the desired service is added, it is displayed in the **Services** list box.
Update/Remove	Displays the **Update or Remove Services** dialog box that enables you to update or remove unnecessary reference books from the **Services** list box.
Parental Control	Enables you to restrict the search options in the **Research** task pane. Protecting the research options by setting a password in the **Parental Control** dialog box prevents unauthorized users from accessing the research services.
Properties	Displays the **Service Properties** dialog box that contains information about the name of the reference book, its description, copyright details, and the name of its provider. The **Properties** button is active only after a particular reference book is selected from the **Services** list box.
The **Favorite** button	Searches for information from the service selected as favorite.

The Translate Feature

Word allows you to select text in a document and translate it into a language of your choice. The *Translation* feature enables you to select text in the document and send it to an online translation service. You can translate selected text using the **Research** pane or use the Mini Translator. You can customize the translation options in the **Research** task pane.

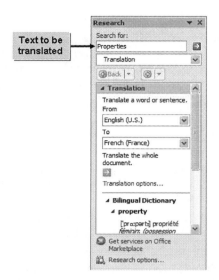

Figure 6-8: *The Research task pane displaying options to translate text.*

How to Use the Thesaurus

Procedure Reference: Select Synonyms or Antonyms from the Thesaurus

To select synonyms or antonyms from the thesaurus:

1. Select the desired word.

 Be sure that the word is spelled correctly. Word will only suggest synonyms for the words in its dictionary.

2. Display the synonyms and antonyms in the **Research** task pane.

    ● Right-click the selected word for which you want to find a synonym or antonym and choose **Synonyms→Thesaurus** or;

    ● On the **Review** tab, in the **Proofing** group, click **Thesaurus** or;

    ● Hold down **Alt** and double-click the desired word or;

    ● Press **Shift+F7.**

3. In the **Research** task pane, in the **Thesaurus: English (U.S.)** list box, point to the desired synonym or antonym, click the drop-down arrow, and then select **Insert** to replace the existing word.

 If you accidentally click the word, just click the **Previous Search** or **Back** button to return to the previous list of options.

4. If necessary, as you type in the document, right-click a word, choose **Synonyms,** and from the displayed menu, choose a synonym.

Procedure Reference: Change the Research Options

To change the research options:

1. Select the **Review** tab, and in the **Proofing** group, click **Research.**

2. In the **Research** task pane, click **Research options.**

3. In the **Research Options** dialog box, change the research options.

   - In the **Services** list box, check or uncheck the desired check box to display or hide the corresponding service option in the **Research** task pane.

   - Add the desired service to the available services.

     a. In the **Research Options** dialog box, click **Add Services.**

     b. In the **Add Services** dialog box, in the **Address** text box, type the URL of an Office 2010 compatible service, or in the **Advertised services** list, select an advertised service.

     c. Click **Add** and follow the instructions.

   - If necessary, insert a password to restrict the display of content in the **Research** task pane.

     a. In the **Research Options** dialog box, click **Parental Control.**

     b. In the **Parental Control** dialog box, check the **Turn on content filtering to make services block offensive results** check box to activate the **Specify a password for the parental control settings** section.

     c. In the **Specify a password for the parental control settings** text box, enter a password and click **OK.**

     d. In the **Research Options** dialog box, click **OK.**

ACTIVITY 6-3
Using the Thesaurus to Replace a Word

Before You Begin:
The My OGC Properties.docx file is open.

Scenario:
While reviewing the OGC Properties document, you find that some words have been used repeatedly. You want to avoid this repetition and replace those words with similar ones. Additionally, you decide to add a research service to the **Research Options** dialog box in Word to quickly complete the necessary research while creating the document.

1. Replace the word "mainly" in the second paragraph with its synonym "primarily."

   a. Scroll up to the first page, and in the second paragraph, in the fourth line, right-click the word "mainly."

   b. In the displayed menu, choose **Synonyms→primarily.**

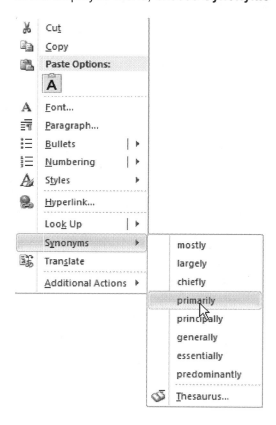

2. Replace the word "aim" in the fourth paragraph with the word "goal."

   a. Scroll down to the end of the first page.

b. In the first line of text below the title "Our Goal," right-click the word "aim," and choose **Synonyms**→ **Thesaurus.**

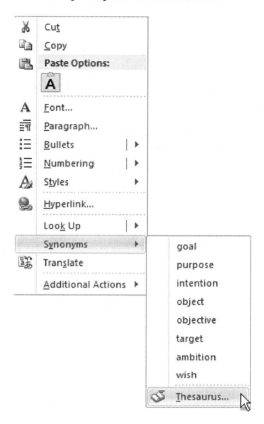

c. In the **Research** task pane, in the **Thesaurus: English (U.S.)** list box, place the mouse pointer over the word "goal," click the drop-down arrow, and then select **Insert.**

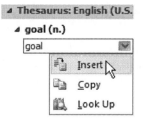

3. Add a service to Word's research options.

a. In the **Research** task pane, click the **Research options** link.

b. In the **Research Options** dialog box, click **Add Services.**

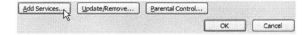

c.   In the **Add Services** dialog box, in the **Address** text box, type ***http:// integrate.factiva.com/research/query.asmx*** and click **Add.**

d.   In the **Factiva, from Dow Jones Setup** dialog box, click **Continue** and click **Install.**

e.   In the **Add Services** message box, click **OK.**

f.   In the **Research Options** dialog box, in the **Services** list box, scroll down, verify that the **Factiva iWorks™** check box is checked, and click **OK.**

g.   Close the **Research** task pane.

h.   Save and close the file.

Lesson 6 Follow-up

In this lesson, you used several proofing tools to make documents more accurate. These tools can assist you with the mechanics of data entry and data revision so that you can concentrate on the creative aspects of writing to produce clear, accurate, and interesting documents.

1. **Which proofing tools do you think you will tend to use most often?**

2. **How do you think the proofing tools will help you in creating professional documents?**

7 | **Controlling the Appearance of Pages in a Word Document**

Lesson Time: 45 minutes

Lesson Objectives:

In this lesson, you will control the appearance of pages in a Word document.

You will:

● Apply a page border and color.

● Add a watermark.

● Add headers and footers.

Introduction

You proofed a Word document for accuracy. Now, you want to add the finishing touches to the document by adjusting the appearance of pages in a document. In this lesson, you will control the appearance of pages in a Word document.

Altering the appearance of a page to suit its content helps you create more professional documents. A formal letter looks best with a simple border, whereas a certificate looks good with a colorful border. By using a variety of options, you can enhance the appearance of pages and improve the presentation of a document.

TOPIC A
Apply a Page Border and Color

You checked a document for spelling and grammar errors to make it accurate. Along with accurate content, you will also need to ensure that the overall appearance of document pages is enhanced to captivate the attention of the readers. In this topic, you will apply a border and color to pages in a Word document.

A document with only plain text and tables, without any color element in it, can at times be very bland. Colored and bordered pages not only add visual interest to a document, but also make the content stand out clearly and help the readers focus on the more important ideas.

Page Borders

Definition:

Page borders are outlines that are applied around the pages of a document. They can be of any style, color, or width. Borders can be applied either to the document as a whole, to a specific section, or only in the margin area of a document. Just as you can add borders, you can also remove borders from a document.

Example:

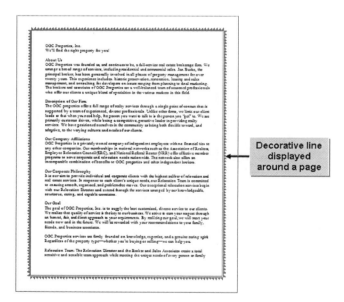

Figure 7-1: *Borders applied to a page and a paragraph.*

Border Types

Word provides you with two types of borders: Line and Art. Line page borders are the default border styles, whereas numerous seasonal and professional Art page borders serve as printed frames for certificates, awards, or diplomas.

Border Type	Description
line 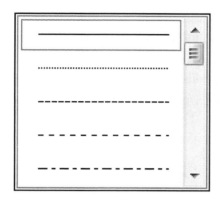	When you select this border type, it is either applied as a line or with a custom style, where you can choose a border style from a list of styles. The style, color, and width of the line in the border can be modified.
art 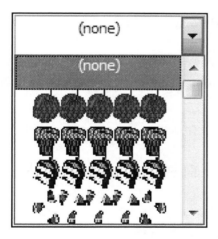	When you select this border type, it is either applied as a box or with a custom style, where you can choose a border style from a list of styles. The size and color of the art in the border can also be modified.

The Page Color Option

The *Page Color* option is used to apply a color shade to the background of a page. You can apply any shade to the page by choosing a color from the **Page Color** gallery. You can also apply a custom color as a page background.

How to Apply a Page Border and Color

Procedure Reference: Apply a Page Border

To apply a border to a page:

1. Select the page in which the border needs to be displayed.
2. Display the **Page Border** tab of the **Borders and Shading** dialog box.
   - On the **Home** tab, in the **Paragraph** group, from the **Borders** drop-down list, select **Borders and Shading,** and in the **Borders and Shading** dialog box, select the **Page Border** tab or;
   - On the **Page Layout** tab, in the **Page Background** group, click **Page Borders.**
3. Set the border options.
   - Specify the desired settings, style, color, and width settings for a line page border.
   - From the **Art** drop-down list, select an art border and set the color and width options.
4. If necessary, in the **Preview** area, click the Border buttons to add or remove borders.
5. Click **OK** to apply the border.

Procedure Reference: Apply a Page Color

To apply color to a page:

1. On the **Page Layout** tab, in the **Page Background** group, click the **Page Color** drop-down arrow.
2. From the **Page Color** gallery, select the desired shade.
3. If necessary, from the Page Color gallery, select **More Colors,** and in the **Colors** dialog box, set a color and click **OK.**

Procedure Reference: Format the Document Background

To format the document background:

1. On the **Page Layout** tab, in the **Paragraph** group, click the **Page Color** drop-down arrow.
2. From the displayed gallery, select **Fill Effects.**
3. In the **Fill Effects** dialog box, set a background for the document.
   - Select the **Gradient** tab, and choose colors, transparency, and shading style for a gradient background.
   - Select the **Texture** tab, and choose a pre-defined texture or insert an image as a texture.
   - Select the **Pattern** tab, and select pattern and colors to be applied to the background and foreground of the pattern.
   - Select the **Picture** tab, and insert a picture as the page background.
4. In the **Fill Effects** dialog box, click **OK** to apply the changes.

ACTIVITY 7-1

Applying an Art Page Border

Data Files:

C:\084582Data\Controlling the Appearance of Pages in a Word Document\Certificate.docx

Scenario:

The content of a sales certificate you have created is approved by your manager. You now have to make the certificate visually impressive when presented to the employees. Your company has installed a new color printer, and you decide to make the certificate colorful to enhance its visual appeal.

---

1. Apply an Art page border to the top and bottom of the page.

    a. On the Quick access toolbar, click **Open.**

    b. From the C:\084582Data\Controlling the Appearance of Pages in a Word Document folder, open the Certificate.docx file.

    c. On the **Page Layout** tab, in the **Page Background** group, click **Page Borders.**

    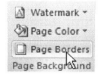

    d. In the **Borders and Shading** dialog box, on the **Page Border** tab, in the **Art** drop-down list, scroll down and select the Music notes border.

    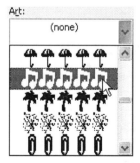

e. From the **Color** drop-down list, in the **Standard Colors** section, select **Blue,** which is the third shade from the right.

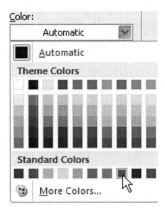

f. Click the Left and Right border buttons to remove the bordering applied on the respective sides.

g. Click **OK** to apply the art border and close the dialog box.

2. Apply a background color to the certificate.

a. On the **Page Layout** tab, in the **Page Background** group, click the **Page Color** drop-down arrow.

b. In the Page Color gallery, in the **Theme Colors** section, select **Dark Blue, Text 2, Lighter 80%** which is the fourth color from left in the second row.

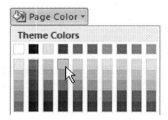

c. Select the **File** tab and choose **Print.**

d. Observe the changes to the layout of the certificate in the preview pane.

e. Save the document as *My Certificate* in the DOCX format, and close the file.

TOPIC B
Add a Watermark

You added page borders and applied colors to pages. Another element that can be added to pages in a Word document is a watermark. In this topic, you will add a watermark to a document.

Sometimes, a document may need to carry a warning or informational message that is displayed throughout the document to prevent the document from being copied. To ensure that the message cannot be omitted in copies, it has to appear with the content and not separately in the margins of the document. For example, you may need to protect your intellectual property by ensuring that the word "Copyright" is displayed on any photocopy of the document. There may also be a legal requirement that requires you to differentiate confidential information from information that is publicly available. Adding watermarks enables you to meet these requirements, protect the information, and produce professional-looking document outputs.

Watermarks

Definition:

A *watermark* is transparent text or a graphic that appears behind the primary content in a document. Watermarks are displayed when the document is printed or previewed. Once you add a watermark, it is automatically applied to the whole document. You can also delete or customize an existing watermark.

Example:

Figure 7-2: Text watermark applied to a document.

The Printed Watermark Dialog Box

The **Printed Watermark** dialog box contains options for creating and customizing watermarks in a document. You can select a picture to use as a picture watermark, scale the picture, and adjust its transparency. You can also specify the text and font appearance for watermarks and determine whether the watermark should run diagonally or horizontally.

How to Add a Watermark

Procedure Reference: Add a Watermark

To add a watermark:

1. On the **Page Layout** tab, in the **Page Background** group, click the **Watermark** drop-down arrow.
2. In the Watermark gallery, select one of the default watermarks, or click **Custom Watermark.**
3. In the **Printed Watermark** dialog box, specify the watermark settings.
   - Specify a text watermark.
      a. Select the **Text watermark** option.
         - From the **Language** drop-down list, select a language.
         - From the **Text** drop-down list, select a text for the watermark to be used.
         - From the **Font** drop-down list, select the font style.
         - From the **Size** drop-down list, select the font size.
         - From the **Color** drop-down list, select a text color.
         - In the **Layout** section, select either **Diagonal** or **Horizontal** orientation.
   - Specify an image watermark.
      a. Select the **Picture watermark** option.
      b. Click the **Select Picture** button.
      c. In the **Insert Picture** dialog box, select the picture to be added as a watermark, and click **Insert.**
   - Select the **No watermark** option, if you do not want to use watermarks in the document.
4. Click **Apply** and **OK** to apply the changes and close the **Printed Watermark** dialog box.

ACTIVITY 7-2
Adding a Text Watermark

Data Files:

C:\084582Data\Controlling the Appearance of Pages in a Word Document\OGC Properties.docx

Scenario:

The document that you created is ready to be reviewed. However, the last time you sent something for review, it was printed without your approval and several copies had to be thrown away. To avoid such wastage, you decide to mark the document as an "INTERNAL DRAFT" so that there is no question about the document's current status.

---

1. Display the **Printed Watermark** dialog box.

   a. On the Quick access toolbar, click **Open.**

   b. From the C:\084582Data\Controlling the Appearance of the Pages in a Word Document folder, open the OGC Properties.docx file.

   c. Select the **Page Layout** tab, and in the **Page Background** group, from the **Watermark** drop-down arrow, select **Custom Watermark.**

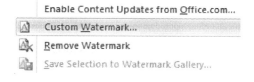

---

2. Apply the text "INTERNAL DRAFT" as a watermark.

   a. In the **Printed Watermark** dialog box, select the **Text watermark** option.

   b. In the **Text** text box, double-click the text "ASAP," which is displayed by default, to select it, and type **INTERNAL DRAFT**

   c. In the **Font** drop-down list, scroll up and select **Arial.**

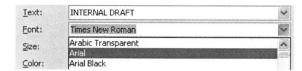

   d. Click **OK** to add the text watermark to the document's background.

   e. Observe that the text watermark is added to the document.

   f. Save the document.

TOPIC C
Add Headers and Footers

You added watermarks to a Word document. Another way to add repetitive information in a document is to add headers and footers. In this topic, you will add headers and footers in a Word document.

Certain information such as page numbers, author names, or chapter titles may need to consistently appear in every page of a document. Rather than typing such information in each page, you can add it once in a document and ensure that it is displayed on all the pages so that you can save time.

Headers and Footers

Headers and *footers* are defined areas below the top and above the bottom margins of a page where you can add textual or graphical information that is common to all or to some of the pages in a document. Common information such as titles, dates, and page numbers can be entered in the **Left, Center,** or **Right** section of a header and footer. You can add header or footer content that is unique to just the first page of a document. You can also apply different header and footer content to odd and even numbered pages.

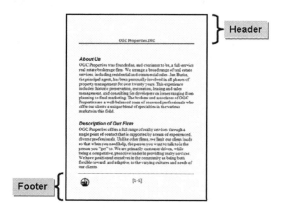

Figure 7-3: A header and footer added to a page.

Fields

A field is a placeholder for data that is used to dynamically represent information such as the current date, time, or page number. Although fields are normally inserted in the header and footer sections of a document, they can be inserted between the content too. When the insertion point is within a field, the field's background turns gray to help identify it as a field. Usually, a field is automatically updated, based on the information provided. To manually update a field, you can press **F9.** The **Field** dialog box enables you to quickly insert fields.

The Header and Footer Tools Design Contextual Tab

The **Header and Footer Tools Design** contextual tab contains various groups that help you work with headers and footers.

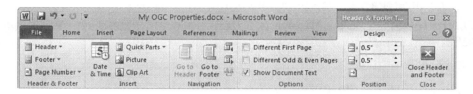

Figure 7-4: *The Header and Footer Tools Design contextual tab displaying commands for working with headers and footers.*

Group	Description
Header & Footer	Contains built-in header, footer, and page number styles that can be used to format headers and footers.
Insert	Contains options that enable you to insert objects, such as pictures and clip arts, in headers and footers. You can also insert the date and time by using the options in this group.
Navigation	Contains options to navigate to header, footer, and previous or next sections in a document.
Options	Contains options to apply different formatting to header or footer on the first page, on odd and even pages, or to the entire document.
Position	Contains options to modify the size of header and footer area. This group also allows you to align the content of the header and footer.
Close	Contain option that enable you to close header or footer section and return to the normal view of the document.

How to Add Headers and Footers

Procedure Reference: Add Headers and Footers in a Document

To add headers and footers in a document:

1. Display the header and footer section.

    - Double-click either the top or bottom of the text area in a document, or;

    - On the **Insert** tab, in the **Header & Footer** group, click **Header** or **Footer** and select **Edit Header** or **Edit Footer** respectively.

2. Insert the header or footer text.

    - In the **Header** or **Footer** section, type the text.

    - If necessary, align the text to the center, left, or to the right of the header or footer section.

    - Insert a built-in header or footer.

        - Insert a built in header.

            a. On the **Insert** tab, in the **Header & Footer** group, click the **Header** drop-down arrow.

            b. From the **Built-In** section, choose a header of your choice to insert in the document.

        - Insert a built-in footer.

            a. On the **Insert** tab, in the **Header & Footer** group, click the **Footer** drop-down arrow.

            b. From the **Built-In** section, choose a footer of your choice to insert in the document.

Custom Dialog Boxes

Though you can enter information manually in headers and footers, Word also provides other features to enter header and footer information. You can change the page number formatting by selecting an option from the Page Number gallery, and insert a clip art using the Clip Art task pane. Content such as date and time, pictures, and quick parts such as fields, building blocks and autotext can be inserted using various dialog boxes. These dialog boxes allow you to specify custom formats and select from pre-built formats for header and footer content.

Procedure Reference: Add Page Numbers to Headers and Footers

To add page numbers:

1. Display the header and footer section.

2. On the **Insert** tab, in the **Header & Footer** group, from the **Page Number** drop-down list, select **Top of Page** or **Bottom of Page,** and then select the desired page number format.

> The **Page Number** drop-down list provides options to insert and modify the page numbers at the top or bottom of pages, or in the left or right margins. You can add custom formats to page numbers or even remove page numbers.

3. If necessary, format the page numbers.

    a. On the **Header & Footer Tools Design** contextual tab, in the **Header & Footer** group, from the **Page Number** drop-down list, select **Format Page Numbers.**

    b. In the **Page Number Format** dialog box, from the **Number format** drop-down list, select the desired format and click **OK** to set the new format and to close the dialog box.

Page Number Format Options

By using the **Header & Footer** group of the **Header & Footer Tools Design** contextual tab, you can change the page number formats from the default "1, 2, 3" format to any of the Arabic or Roman numeral formats that are given below.

- -1-, -2-, -3-, ...
- a, b, c, ...
- A, B, C, ...
- i, ii, iii, ...
- I, II, III, ...

Procedure Reference: Add a Date and Time to the Header or Footer

To add a date and time to the header or footer:

1. Select header or footer in which the date and time need to be included.

2. On the **Header & Footer Tools Design** contextual tab, in the **Insert** group, click **Date & Time.**

3. In the **Date and Time** dialog box, in the **Available formats** list box, select the desired date and time format.

4. If necessary, check the **Update automatically** check box to automatically update the date and time according to the computer's system settings.

5. Click **OK** to insert the date and time, and on the **Header & Footer Tools Design** contextual tab, in the **Close** group, click **Close Header and Footer.**

6. If necessary, double-click the date and time in the header or footer, and in the **Date and Time** dialog box, select a different format to modify the date and time format.

Procedure Reference: Modify Headers or Footers

To modify headers or footers:

1. Double-click the header or footer that you want to modify.

2. On the **Header & Footer Tools Design** contextual tab, set the necessary formatting options.

    - In the **Header & Footer** group, select a built-in format for header or footer.

    - In the **Insert** group, insert the date and time, a picture, or clip art.

    - In the **Navigation** group, select an option to navigate to the desired header or footer in the current document section or another document section.

    - In the **Options** group, specify the format for headers and footers on specific pages.

    - In the **Position** group, set the dimension of header and footer.

3. In the **Close** group, click **Close Header and Footer.**

Procedure Reference: Delete a Header or Footer

To delete a header or footer:

1. Select the **Insert** tab.
2. If necessary, in **Header & Footer** group, from the **Header** drop-down list, select **Remove Header** to remove header from the document.
3. If necessary, in the **Header & Footer** group, from the **Footer** drop-down list, select **Remove Footer** to remove footer from the document.

Procedure Reference: Apply the Different First Page Attribute

To apply different first page attribute:

1. Select header or footer.
2. On the **Header & Footer Tools Design** contextual tab, in the **Options** group, select an option to specify the attributes for header or footer.
   - Check the **Different First Page** check box to apply a different header or footer to the first page.
   - Check **Different Odd & Even Pages** check box to apply different headers and footers to odd and even numbered pages.

Procedure Reference: Navigate Through the Header and Footer

To navigate to header & footer:

1. Select header or footer.
2. On the **Header & Footer Tools Design** contextual tab, in the **Navigation** group
   - Select **Go to Header**, to navigate to a header.
   - Select **Go to Footer**, to navigate to a footer.
   - Select **Previous** or **Next** to navigate to the previous or next section of the document.

ACTIVITY 7-3
Adding Headers and Footers

Before You Begin:

The OGC Properties.docx file is open.

Scenario:

Your manager is giving a presentation at the New World Properties Expo conference, and wants to leave behind the company's overview as a handout so that potential clients can peruse last year's successes. Your job is to make the handout more identifiable as an OGC Properties document. You realize that to accomplish this, it will be helpful if the company's name is displayed on the handout in addition to the page numbers and the current date and time. You are also informed by your manager to draw special attention to the first page of the document.

1. Insert the text "OGC Properties" in the center placeholder of the header.

   a. Double-click the top of the document to display the header and footer sections.

   b. Press **Tab** to move the insertion point to the center of the header section.

   c. Type **OGC PROPERTIES**

2. Add a footer that includes the current date and time, the conference name, and the page number.

   a. On the **Header and Footer Tools Design** contextual tab, in the **Header & Footer** group, in the **Page Number** drop-down list, and select **Bottom of Page** and then select **Accent Bar 4.**

   b. In the footer section, type **New World Properties Expo** and press **Tab** to move the text to the center placeholder.

   c. On the **Header & Footer Tools Design** contextual tab, in the **Insert** group, click **Date & Time.**

   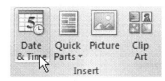

d. In the **Date and Time** dialog box, in the **Available formats** list box, select the twelfth format that includes both the date and time.

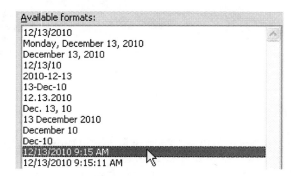

e. Click **OK** to insert the selected date and time format.

f. Press **Tab** to center the date and time.

3. Add a different header and footer on the first page.

a. On the **Header & Footer Tools Design** contextual tab, in the **Options** group, check the **Different First Page** check box.

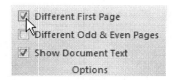

b. In the **Navigation** group, click **Go to Header.**

c. On the **Header and Footer Tools Design** contextual tab, in the **Header & Footer** group, from the **Header** drop-down list, select **Alphabet.**

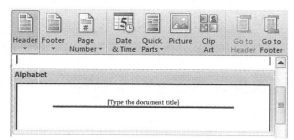

d. In the header section, place the insertion point before the text " About Us" triple-click the text and type *OVERVIEW OF OGC PROPERTIES*

e. On the **Header and Footer Tools Design** contextual tab, in the **Header & Footer** group, from the **Footer** drop-down list, select **Alphabet.**

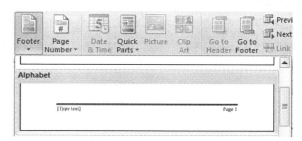

f. Click the text "Type text" and type *NEW WORLD PROPERTIES EXPO*

g. On the **Header & Footer Tools Design** contextual tab, in the **Close** group, click **Close Header and Footer.**

4. Preview the content of the new header and footer.

a. Select the **View** tab, and in the **Zoom** group, click **One Page.**

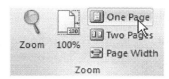

b. On the **View** tab, in the **Zoom** group, click **100%**

c. Scroll down to the bottom of the first page.

d. Save the document.

ACTIVITY 7-4
Modifying Headers and Footers

Before You Begin:

The OGC Properties.docx file is open.

Scenario:

As you read through your document, you find that only the first page of the document provides an overview of OGC Properties and the remaining pages include detailed analyses of the company. You want to include the overview information in all the pages of the document, as well as make some modifications to the header and page numbering format.

1. Change header to read "OGC PROPERTIES ANNUAL REPORT."

    a. Scroll down to the second page.

    b. At the top of the second page, double-click the header section to edit the text in the header area.

    c. Place the insertion point at the end of the header text "OGC PROPERTIES," press the **Spacebar,** and type **ANNUAL REPORT**

2. Edit footer to display only the page number at the center.

    a. On the **Header & Footer Tools Design** contextual tab, in the **Navigation** group, click **Go to Footer.**

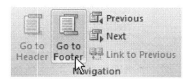

    b. Select all the text in the footer section, except the page number, and press **Delete.**

    c. Press **Tab** to place the insertion point in the center.

d. On the **Header & Footer Tools Design** contextual tab, in the **Header & Footer** group, from the **Page Number** drop-down list, select **Bottom of Page.**

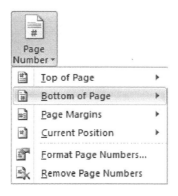

e. In the displayed gallery, in the **Plain Number** section, scroll down, and select **Brackets 1.**

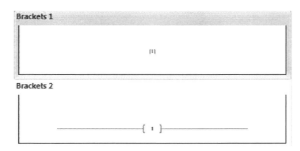

f. On the **Header & Footer Tools Design** contextual tab, in the **Header & Footer** group, from the **Page Number** drop-down list, select **Format Page Numbers.**

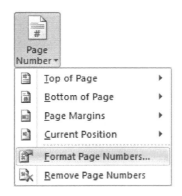

g. In the **Page Number Format** dialog box, from the **Number format** drop-down list, select **–1–, –2–, –3–...**

h. Click **OK** to apply the changes.

    i.   Scroll down to observe the header & footer.

    j.   Observe that the footer is modified.

          [- 1 -]

    k.   On the **Header & Footer Tools Design** contextual tab, in the **Close** group, click **Close Header and Footer.**

    l.   Save and close the document.

Lesson 7 Follow-up

In this lesson, you customized the appearance of pages in a document. Adding headers and footers, applying page borders and colors, and including watermarks will allow you to create professional-looking documents that are complete in all aspects.

1. **How will you make use of the various page layout options to enhance the appearance of a document?**

2. **Considering how you work, do you attempt to modify the page setup options of a document when you create a document or wait until you are almost finished with the document? Why?**

8 | Printing Word Documents

Lesson Time: 30 minutes

Lesson Objectives:

In this lesson, you will print a Word document.

You will:

- Control page layout.
- Preview and print a document.

Introduction

You controlled the appearance of pages in a Word document. You may now want to ensure that the pages print as they were intended to be printed. In this lesson, you will print Word documents.

Printing a document may work out to be expensive if you repeatedly print multi-page documents just to see how it will look on paper, or to do a quick hard copy edit. By previewing a document before printing it, and ensuring that its page settings are as desired, and by identifying obvious errors, you can be assured that the output will be as expected without wasting resources and time.

TOPIC A
Control Page Layout

You finalized the appearance of pages in a Word document. Adjusting various aspects of the overall page layout is another task that will allow you to adjust the appearance of document pages when they are printed. In this topic, you will control the layout of a page.

Very often, the way a document is displayed on screen is not the way it is displayed in the printed output. Just as an architect decides on the layout for a new house by keeping in mind the visual appeal and the owner's needs, defining the layout of documents before they are printed ensures that the content will be displayed as you want it to. Word allows you to specify page margins and orientation which ensures that the printed output meets your requirements.

Margin Options

The Margins gallery, accessible from the **Page Setup** group of the **Page Layout** tab, has a list of predefined margin types. You can select a predefined margin type and apply it to a document to change the top, bottom, left, and right margins in the document. Inside and outside margins refer to the edges of the pages inside a binding, if the document is compiled in the form of a book. Generally, the inside edge is the left edge for right hand pages and vice versa. You can also individually customize the size of each margin to increase or decrease the text area, add white space, or adjust the overall layout of the page.

Default Margin Types

Word has six default margin types. Each margin type sets different dimensions for the various margins in a document.

Margin Type	Description
Normal	Top, bottom, left, and right margins are at a distance of 1 inch from the page border.
Narrow	Top, bottom, left, and right margins are at a distance of 0.5 inches from the page border.
Moderate	Top and bottom margins are at a distance of 1 inch, and left and right margins are at a distance of 0.75 inches from the page border.
Wide	Top and bottom margins are at a distance of 1 inch, and left and right margins are at a distance of 2 inches from the page border.
Mirrored	Top and bottom margins are at a distance of 1 inch, inside margins are at a distance of 1.25 inches, and outside margins are at a distance of 1 inch from the page border.
Office 2003 Default	Top and bottom margins are at a distance of 1 inch, and left and right margins are at a distance of 1.25 inches from the page border.

Vertical Alignment Options

You can control how the text on a page is aligned vertically between the top and bottom margins. The options are similar to the horizontal alignment options that are available for paragraph formatting. The vertical alignment options work the same way for both the portrait and landscape page orientation.

Vertical Alignment Option	Description
Top	Positions the text along the top margin of a page. It is the default vertical alignment setting.
Center	Positions the text in the center of a page, providing equal amounts of white space above and below the text.
Justified	Adds equal amounts of white space between each paragraph so that the text appears to fill the page.
Bottom	Aligns the text along the bottom margin of a page.

Mirrored Margins

Mirrored margins are used in documents when pages need to be printed and bound, stapled, or filed. They provide more space on the inside margins to allow for the binding, stapling, or filing.

Page Orientation

Definition:

Page orientation is a page setup option that determines how the information on a page will be laid out. In portrait orientation, page content is laid out vertically with the height of the page being greater than the width. In landscape orientation, content is laid out horizontally, with the width of the page being greater than its height. The orientation setting affects the overall layout of text on a page and the printing of a document.

Example:

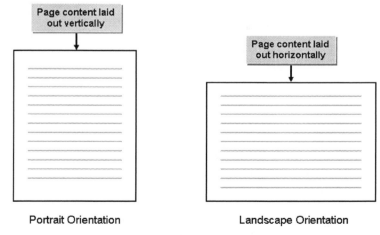

Portrait Orientation   Landscape Orientation

Figure 8-1: Document displayed in Portrait and Landscape Orientation.

The Paper Size Option

Paper size option allows you to modify the width and height of a document appropriate to the paper that is used for printing. In Word, the **Size** drop-down list contains various paper sizes that are used to resize a document. It can be accessed from the **Page Setup** group of the **Page Layout** tab. You can also specify a custom paper size by selecting the **More Paper Sizes** option and specifying the settings in the **Page Setup** dialog box.

Paper Size Options

The **Size** drop-down list contains a number of default paper sizes. Each size has a predefined width and height, specified in inches. The sizes correspond to the standard sizes of papers and envelopes that are commonly used in business correspondence in various countries and geographic regions.

Paper Size	Width in Inches	Height in Inches
Letter	8.5	11
Legal	8.5	14
Executive	7.25	10.5
A4	8.27	11.69
B5 (JIS)	7.17	10.12
Envelope #10	4.12	9.5
Envelope DL	4.33	8.66
Envelope C5	6.38	9.02
Envelope B5	6.93	9.84
Envelope Monarch	3.88	7.5

The Page Setup Dialog Box

The **Page Setup** dialog box has various tabs, which contain options that help you modify the overall layout of pages in a document.

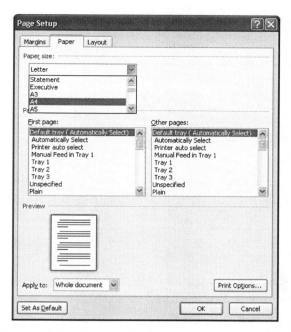

Figure 8-2: *The Page Setup dialog box displaying options in the Paper tab.*

Page Setup Tab	Description
Margins	Enables you to set margins and page orientation. It also contains options to specify whether the settings are to be applied to the whole document or to specific pages.
Paper	Allows you to modify the paper size and paper source for printing. It also enables you to access the **Display** tab in the **Word Options** dialog box to customize the display settings of the document.
Layout	Enables you to modify the layout of a particular section and set different styles for the page borders.

Page Breaks

Definition:

A *page break* is a marking available in an electronic document which splits the content across pages at the specific location. When there is too much text that needs to be fit on a page, an automatic soft page break is inserted at the end of each page to move text to the next page. However, you can also insert a page break to control where a page ends.

 Automatic soft page breaks are primarily determined by the margin settings in the **Page Setup** dialog box. Automatic page breaks display differently in the different document views.

Example:

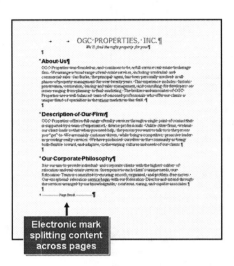

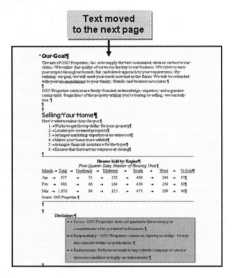

Figure 8-3: *A Page break applied to a document.*

White Space Between Pages

There is an extra white space at the bottom of the page where a break is inserted. Show/Hide White space also hides the top and bottom margins of the pages to enable easier scrolling when you are in the **Print Layout** view. When you position the mouse pointer between the two pages, the mouse pointer changes to a Hide White Space or Show White Space pointer. You can toggle between the Hide White Space and Show White Space modes by double-clicking or holding down **Ctrl** while clicking between the pages.

How to Control Page Layout

Procedure Reference: Insert a Manual Page Break

To insert a manual page break:

1. Insert a manual page break.

   - On the **Page Layout** tab, in the **Page Setup** group, from the **Breaks** drop-down list, select **Page** or;
   - Press **Ctrl+Enter.**

2. If necessary, delete a page break.

   - Click after the page break and press **Backspace** or;
   - Click before the page break and press **Delete.**

Procedure Reference: Control the Layout of a Page

To control the layout of a page:

1. Open the document in which the page layout needs to be changed.
2. Change the page orientation.

   - On the **Page Layout** tab, in the **Page Setup** group, click **Orientation** and select **Portrait** or **Landscape** or;
   - Change the page orientation by using the **Page Setup** dialog box.

a. On the **Page Layout** tab, in the **Page Setup** group, click the **Page Setup** dialog box launcher.

b. In the **Page Setup** dialog box, on the **Margins** tab, in the **Orientation** section, select **Portrait** or **Landscape** to position the page vertically or horizontally, respectively and click **OK.**

3. Set the paper size.

- On the **Page Layout** tab, in the **Page Setup** group, from the **Size** drop-down list, select a size or;

- In the **Page Setup** dialog box, select the **Paper** tab, and from the **Paper size** drop-down list, select a paper size and click **OK** or;

- In the **Page Setup** dialog box, select the **Paper** tab, and in the **Paper size** section, in the **Width** and **Height** text boxes, enter the custom values and click **OK.**

4. Set the page margins.

- On the **Page Layout** tab, in the **Page Setup** group, from the **Margins** drop-down list, select an option.

- Drag the margin markers on the vertical and horizontal rulers. Hold down **Alt** as you drag to set an exact measurement.

- Open the **Page Setup** dialog box, and on the **Margins** tab, specify the measurements for the **Top, Bottom, Left,** and **Right** margins in their respective spin boxes and click **OK.**

5. Set the vertical alignment.

a. Open the **Page Setup** dialog box and select the **Layout** tab.

b. In the **Page** section, from the **Vertical alignment** drop-down list, select an alignment and click **OK.**

ACTIVITY 8-1
Inserting Manual Page Breaks

Data Files:

C:\084582Data\Printing Word Documents\OGC Properties.docx

Scenario:

The editor of the annual report has handed off the stockholders' reports to you. You need to include the information from those reports in the OGC Properties document. The problem is that the pages are breaking in places where you do not want them to, resulting in separating data that really needs to stay together. After you adjust the page breaks, you want to quickly scroll through the document to check the overall text flow from page to page to see if there are any pages that you should combine.

---

1. Insert a manual page break before the heading " REVIEW OF YEAR RESULTS " and above the heading "Rates of Interest."

   a. On the **Quick Access** toolbar, click **Open**.

   b. From theC:\084582Data\Printing Word Documentsfolder, open the OGC Properties.docx file.

   c. Observe the status bar to verify that there are currently ten pages in the document.

   d. Scroll down to the fifth page and place the insertion point before the heading "REVIEW OF YEAR RESULTS."

   e. Select the **Page Layout** tab, and in the **Page Setup** group, from the **Breaks** drop-down list, select **Page.**

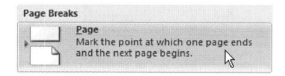

   f. Scroll down to the end of page 8.

   g. On page 8, place the insertion point before the picture.

   h. On the **Page Layout** tab, in the **Page Setup** group, from the **Breaks** drop-down list, select **Page.**

---

2. Hide the top and bottom margins of pages.

   a. Position the insertion point between pages 8 and 9 to display the Hide White Space pointer.

   b. Double-click between the pages to hide the top and bottom margins.

    c.   Verify that you can see continuous text without headers and footers.

3.   Display the top and bottom margins.

    a.   Scroll up to the end of page 6.

    b.   Position the insertion point between pages 6 and 7 to display the Show White Space pointer.

    c.   Double-click the line separating the pages to display the top and bottom margins and whitespace at the end of the pages.

    d.   Save the file as **My OGC Properties** in the DOCX format and close it.

ACTIVITY 8-2

Changing the Layout of a Document

Data Files:

C:\084582Data\Printing Word Documents\Certificate.docx

Before You Begin:

Ensure that a printer driver is installed.

Scenario:

You are assigned the task of creating a sales certificate. Your manager has provided you with the text and requested that you print the certificate horizontally on A4 paper. Also, you are instructed to include at least 1.5 inches of blank space at the top and bottom of the certificate. Additionally, you want to neatly align the content in the certificate.

---

1. Set the orientation of the document to **Landscape.**

    a. On the **Quick Access** toolbar, click **Open**.

    b. From the C:\084582Data\Controlling the Appearance of the Pages in a Word Documentfolder, open theCertificate.docx file.

    c. Select the **Page Layout** tab, and in the **Page Setup** group, from the **Orientation** drop-down list [🔲 Orientation ▾], select **Landscape.**

    d. Select the **View** tab, in the **Zoom** group, click **Zoom.**

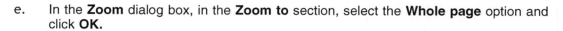

e. In the **Zoom** dialog box, in the **Zoom to** section, select the **Whole page** option and click **OK.**

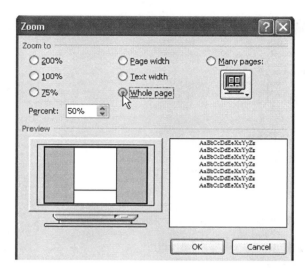

---

2. Set the top and bottom margins of the document to 1.5 inches.

   a. Select the **Page Layout** tab, and in the **Page Setup** group, click the **Page Setup** dialog box launcher.

   b. In the **Page Setup** dialog box , in the **Top** text box `Top:` `1.5"`, type **1.5,** and press **Tab.**

   c. In the **Bottom** text box `Bottom:` `1.5"`, type **1.5.**

---

3. Change the size of the paper to A4.

   a. In the **Page Setup** dialog box, select the **Paper** tab.

   b. From the **Paper size** drop-down list, select **A4.**

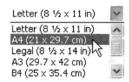

---

4. Center the text vertically on the page.

   a. In the **Page Setup** dialog box, select the **Layout** tab.

b. In the **Page** section, from the **Vertical alignment** drop-down list, select **Center** and click **OK.**

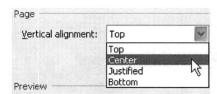

c. Select the **File** tab and choose **Print.**

d. Observe the layout of the certificate in the preview pane.

e. Save the file as **My Certificate** in the DOCX format.

TOPIC B

Preview and Print a Document

You controlled the layout of pages in a document to define their appearance when they are printed. You may now need a printed copy of the document, but before you print the document, it is smart to preview it and check to ensure that it looks the way you intended it to be when printed. In this topic, you will preview and print a Word document.

Printing a document is expensive. Each page may cost only a few cents for paper and ink, but this quickly adds up if you are repeatedly printing a multi-page document just to see how it will look on paper or to do a quick hard copy edit. By previewing a document before printing it, you can still see how it will look and identify obvious errors, without wasting resources and the time it will take to print additional copies.

The Print Option

The **Print** option in Word is integrated into the Backstage view. The Backstage view displays a left pane with options to specify print options and printer settings, and a right pane that displays a preview of the document. The right pane contains the **Zoom** slider and options to view the next and previous pages.

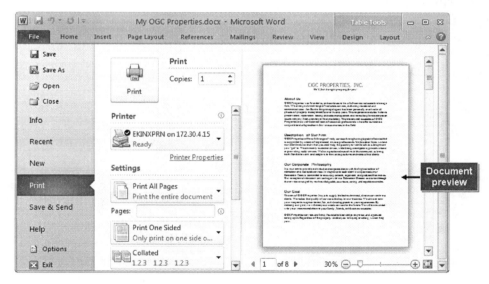

Figure 8-4: *The Print section displaying the preview of a page in a document.*

The left pane contains sections with options for specifying various print document settings.

Section	Description
Print	Print a document or set the number of copies that need to be printed.
Printer	Select a printer from the list of available printers. It also allows you to set printer properties by using the **Printer Properties** link.
Settings	Select the range of pages that need to be printed, set the page orientation, select a paper size, and set margins.

How to Preview and Print a Document

Procedure Reference: Preview a Document

To preview a document:

1. Open a document.
2. Select the **File** tab and choose **Print.**
3. If necessary, use the **Zoom** slider to view the document at the desired magnification level.
4. Click the **Next Page** or **Previous Page** buttons to navigate through the pages in the document preview.

Procedure Reference: Print a Document

To print a document:

1. Open a document.
2. Select the **File** tab and choose **Print.**
3. In the Backstage view, in the **Print** section, specify the number of copies that need to be printed.
4. In the **Printer** section, select a printer and set the printer properties.
5. In the **Settings** section, specify the print settings.
6. Click **Print** to print the document.

ACTIVITY 8-3
Printing a Document

Before You Begin:
1. The My Certificate.docx file is open.
2. Ensure that the necessary print drivers are installed on your computer.

Scenario:
You need to print the certificate that you have created for presentation to the outstanding employees of your company. Before printing, you want to preview the document to verify that the document looks as desired.

---

1. Print the certificate.

    a. Select the **File** tab and choose **Print.**

    b. In the Backstage view, in the **Print** section, click **Print** to print the certificate.

    c. Close the document.

---

2. Preview a document by using different zoom levels.

    a. On the **Quick Access** toolbar, click **Open**.

    b. Navigate to the C:\084582Data\Printing Word Documents folder and open the MY OGC Properties docx file.

    c. Select the **File** tab and choose **Print.**

    d. In the Backstage view, in the right pane, observe that a preview of the document is displayed.

    e. Click the **Zoom In** button to magnify the document.

    f. Click the **Zoom Out** button to view the document at the default magnification level.

---

3. View the other pages in the document.

    a. Click the **Next Page** button to preview the next page of the document.

    b. Click **50%** to display the **Zoom** dialog box.

    c.   In the **Zoom** dialog box, in the **Zoom to** section, select the **Many pages** option and click **OK** to view multiple pages.

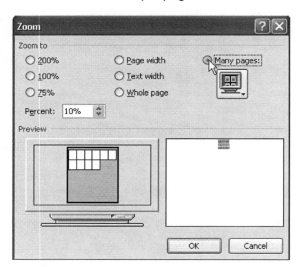

---

4.   Print two copies of the entire document.

    a.   In the **Print** section, in the **Copies** spin box, click the up arrow once to change the value to 2.

    b.   Click **Print** to print the document.

---

5.   Print a copy of the "Rates of Interest" page.

    a.   Select the **File** tab and choose **Print.**

    b.   In the **Print** section, in the **Copies** spin box ⬚, click the down arrow button to change the value to **1**

    c.   In the **Settings** section, in the **Pages** text box, click and type *9*

          Pages: 9

    d.   Click **Print** to print only the ninth page.

    e.   Close the document.

    f.   Select the **File** tab and choose **Exit** to close the application.

Lesson 8 Follow-up

In this lesson, you printed a Word document. Setting up a document for printing and ensuring that it is error-free will allow you to output copies that appear as intended.

1. **How will you make use of the various page layout options to enhance a printed document?**

2. **Which print settings do you expect to frequently specify when printing Word documents? Why?**

Follow-up

In this course you created, edited, and enhanced standard documents using Microsoft® Office Word 2010. These skills will enable you to create professional-looking documents.

1. **Which feature in Word will help the most as you create documents?**

2. **What are the uses of automatic features in Word?**

What's Next?

Microsoft® Office Word 2010: Level 2 will be the next course in this series.

A Microsoft Office Word 2010

Selected Element K courseware addresses Microsoft Office Specialist (MOS) and MOS Expert certification skills for Microsoft Word 2010. The following table indicates where Word 2010 skills are covered. For example, 3-A indicates the lesson and topic number applicable to that skill, and 3-1 indicates the lesson and activity number.

Objective Domain	Level	Topic	Activity
1. Apply different views to a document.			
1.1 1 Select zoom options	1	1–C	1–3
1.1.2 Split windows	1	1–C	1–3
1.1.3 Arrange windows			
1.1.3.1 View Side by Side	1	1–C	1–3
1.1.3.2 Synchronous Scrolling	1	1–C	
1.1.4 Arrange document views			
1.1.4.1 Reorganize a document outline	3	1–B	
1.1.4.2 Master documents	3	5–F	5–8
1.1.4.3 Subdocuments	3	5–F	5–8
1.1.4.4 Web layout	1	1–C	
1.1.4.5 Draft	1	1–C	
1.1.5 Switch between windows	1	1–C	
1.1.6 Open a document in a new window	1	1–C	
1.2 Apply protection to a document.			
1.2.1 Apply protection by using the Microsoft Office Backstage view commands			
1.2.1.1 Apply controls and restrictions to document access	3	6–F	6–6
1.2.1.2 Password-protect a document	3	6–E	6–5
1.2.1.3 Mark as Final	3	6–F	6–6
1.2.2 Applying protection by using ribbon commands	3	6–F	
1.3 Manage document versions.			
1.3.1 Recover draft versions	1	1–E	

Objective Domain	Level	Topic	Activity
1.3.2 Delete all draft versions	1	1–E	
1.4 Share documents.			
1.4.1 Send documents via E-mail	3	1–C	
1.4.2 Send documents via SkyDrive	3	2–G	
1.4.3 Send documents via Internet fax	3	1–C	
1.4.4 Change file types	1	1–E	
1.4.5 Create PDF documents	1	1–E	
1.4.6 Create	3	Appendix	
1.4.7 Publish a blog post	3	Appendix	
1.4.8 Register a blog account	3	Appendix	
1.5 Save a document.			
1.5.1 Use compatibility mode	1	1–E	
1.5.2 Use protected mode	3	6–C	6–3
1.5.3 Use Save As options	1	1–E	1–5
1.6 Apply a template to a document.			
1.6.1 Find templates			
1.6.1.1 Locate a template on your disk	2	8–A	
1.6.1.2 Find templates on the web	1	1–C	
2.1 Apply font and paragraph attributes.			
2.1.1 Apply character attributes	1	3–A	3–1
2.1.2 Apply styles	1	3–E	3–6
2.1.3 Use Format Painter	1	3–A	3–1
2.2 Navigate and search through a document.			
2.2.1 Use the Navigation Pane	1	2–C	
2.2.1.1 Headings	1	2–C	
2.2.1.2 Pages	1	2–C	
2.2.1.3 Results	1	2–C	
2.2.2 Use Go To	1	2–C	2–3
2.2.3 Use Browse by button	1	2–C	
2.2.4 Use Highlight features	1	3–A	3–2
2.2.5 Set Find and Replace options			
2.2.5.1 Format	1	3–F	
2.2.5.2 Special	1	2–C	
2.3 Apply indentation and tab settings to paragraphs.			
2.3.1 Apply indents			
2.3.1.1 first line	1	3–D	
2.3.1.2 hanging	1	3–D	
2.3.2 Sett tabs	1	3–B	3–3
2.3.3 Use the Tabs dialog box	1	3–B	

Objective Domain	Level	Topic	Activity
2.3.4 Set tabs on the ruler	1	3–B	3–5
2.3.5 Clear tab	1	3–B	
2.3.6 Set tab stops	1	3–B	3–5
2.3.7 Move tab stops	1	3–B	
2.4 Apply spacing settings to text and paragraphs.			
2.4.1 Set line spacing	1	3–D	3–5
2.4.2 Set paragraph spacing	1	3–D	3–5
2.5 Create tables.			
2.5.1 Use the Insert Table dialog box	1	5–A	5–1
2.5.2 Use Draw Table	1	5–A	
2.5.3 Insert a Quick Table	1	5–A	5–1
2.5.4 Convert text to table	1	5–D	5–4
2.5.5 Use a table to control page layout	1	5–A	
2.6 Manipulate tables in a document.			
2.6.1 Sort content	2	2–A	2–1
2.6.2 Add a row to a table	1	5–B	5–2
2.6.3 Add a column to a table	1	5–B	
2.6.4 Manipulate rows			
2.6.4.1 Split	1	5–B	
2.6.4.2 Merge	1	5–B	
2.6.4.3 Move	1	5–B	
2.6.4.4 Resize	1	5–B	
2.6.4.5 Delete	1	5–B	5–2
2.6.5 Manipulate columns			
2.6.5.1 Split	1	5–B	
2.6.5.2 Merge	1	5–B	
2.6.5.3 Move	1	5–B	5–2
2.6.5.4 Resize	1	5–B	5–2
2.6.5.5 Delete	1	5–B	
2.6.6 Define the header row	1	5–C	
2.6.7 Convert tables to text	1	5–D	5–4
2.6.8 View gridlines	1	5–B	
2.7 Apply bullets to a document.			
2.7.1 Apply bullets	1	3–C	
2.7.2 Select a symbol format	1	3–C	
2.7.3 Define a picture to be used as a bullet	2	1–C	
2.7.4 Use AutoFormat	1	3–C	
2.7.5 Promote and demote bullet levels	2	1–C	1–4
3.1 Apply and manipulate page setup settings.			

Objective Domain	Level	Topic	Activity
3.1.1 Set margins	1	3–D, 8–A	8–2
3.1.2 Insert non-breaking spaces	1	3–D	
3.1.3 Add hyphenation	1	3–D	
3.1.4 Add columns	2	7–C	7–3
3.1.5 Remove a break	1	8–A	
3.1.6 Force a page break	1	8–A	8–1
3.1.7 Insert a section break			
3.1.7.1 Continuous	2	7–B	7–2
3.1.7.2 Next page	2	7–B	
3.1.7.3 Next Odd	2	7–B	
3.1.7.4 Next Even	2	7–B	
3.1.8 Insert a blank page into a document	3	5–A	5–1
3.2 Apply themes.			
3.2.1 Use a theme to apply formatting	2	3–C	3–4
3.2.2 Customize a theme	2	3–C	3–4
3.3 Construct content in a document by using the Quick Parts tool.			
3.3.1 Add built-in building blocks			
3.3.1.1 Quotes	2	6–A	
3.3.1.2 Text boxes	2	6–A	
3.3.1.3 Header	2	6–A	
3.3.1.4 Footer	2	6–A	
3.3.1.5 Cover page	2	6–A	
3.3.1.6 Watermark	2	6–A	
3.3.1.7 Equations	2	6–A	
3.4 Create and manipulate page backgrounds.			
3.4.1 Format a document's background	1	7–A	
3.4.2 Set a colored background	1	7–A	7–1
3.4.3 Add a watermark	1	7–B	7–2
3.4.4 Set page borders	1	7–A	7–1
3.5 Create and modify headers and footers.			
3.5.1 Insert page numbers	1	7–C	7–3
3.5.2 Format page numbers	1	7–C	7–4
3.5.3 Insert the current date and time	1	7–C	7–3
3.5.4 Insert a built-in header or footer	1	7–C	
3.5.5 Add content to a header or footer			
3.5.5.1 Custom dialog box	1	7–C	
3.5.5.2 Manual entry	1	7–C	7–3
3.5.6 Delete a header or footer	1	7–C	
3.5.7 Change margins	1	8–A	8–2

Objective Domain	Level	Topic	Activity
3.5.8 Apply a different first page attribute	1	7–C	
4.1 Insert and format pictures in a document.			
4.1.1 Add captions	2	2–D	2–4
4.1.2 Apply artistic effects	2	4–B	4–2
4.1.3 Apply picture styles	2	4–B	
4.1.4 Compress pictures	2	4–B	4–2
4.1.5 Modify a shape	2	5–B	5–3
4.1.6 Adjust position and size	2	4–C	4–3
4.1.7 Insert screenshots	2	4–D	4–4
4.2 Insert and format shapes, WordArt, and SmartArt.			
4.2.1 Add text to a shape	2	5–B	5–3
4.2.2 Modify text on a shape	2	5–D	5–5
4.2.3 Add captions	2	2–D	2–4
4.2.4 Set shape styles			
4.2.4.1 Border	2	5–B	
4.2.4.2 Text	2	5–C	5–4
4.2.5 Adjust position and size	2	5–D	
4.3 Insert and format Clip Art.			
4.3.1 Organize ClipArt	1	4–A	
4.3.2 Add captions	2	2–D	
4.3.3 Apply artistic effects	2	4–B	4–2
4.3.4 Compress pictures	2	4–B	4–2
4.3.5 Adjust position and size	2	4–A	
4.4 Apply and manipulate text boxes.			
4.4.1 Format text boxes	2	5–A	5–1
4.4.2 Save a selection to the text box gallery	2	5–A	
4.4.3 Apply text box styles	2	5–A	5–1
4.4.4 Change Text direction	2	2–B	2–2
4.4.5 Apply shadow effects	2	5–A	5–1
4.4.6 Apply 3-D effects	2	5–A	
5.1 Validate content by using spelling and grammar checking options.			
5.1.1 Set grammar	1	6–A	
5.1.2 Set style options	1	6–A	
5.2 Configure AutoCorrect settings.			
5.2.1 Add or remove exceptions	1	6–A	
5.2.2 Turn on and off AutoCorrect	1	6–A	
5.3 Insert and modify comments in a document			
5.3.1 Insert a comment	3	2–C	2–3

Objective Domain	Level	Topic	Activity
5.3.2 Edit a comment	3	2–C	2–4
5.3.3 Delete a comment	3	2–C	2–4
5.3.4 View a comment			
5.3.4.1 View comments from another user	3	2–F	2–7
5.3.4.2 View comments inline	3	2–F	
5.3.4.3 View comments as balloons	3	2–F	
6.1 Apply a hyperlink.			
6.1.1 Apply a hyperlink to text or graphic	3	4–D	4–4
6.1.2 Use a hyperlink as a bookmark	3	4–D	
6.1.3 Link a hyperlink to an E-mail address	3	4–D	
6.2 Create endnotes and footnotes in a document.			
6.2.1 Demonstrate difference between Endnotes and Footnotes	3	4–B	
6.2.2 Manage footnote and endnote locations	3	4–B	4–2
6.2.3 Configure footnote and endnote format	3	4–B	
6.2.4 Presentation	3	4–B	
6.2.5 Change footnote and endnote numbering	3	4–B	4–2
6.3.1 Use default formats	3	5–E	
6.3.2 Set levels	3	5–E	5–7
6.3.3 Set alignment	3	5–E	
6.3.4 Set tab leader	3	5–E	
6.3.5 Modify styles	3	5–E	5–7
6.3.6 Update a table of contents			
6.3.6.1 Page numbers	3	5–E	
6.3.6.2 Entire table	3	5–E	
7.1 Set up mail merge.			
7.1.1 Perform a mail merge using the Mail Merge Wizard	2	9–A	9–1
7.1.2 Perform a mail merge manually	2	9–A	
7.1.3 Use Auto Check for Errors	2	9–A	9–1
7.2 Execute mail merge.			
7.2.1 Preview and print a mail merge operation	2	9–A	9–1

B Microsoft Office Word Expert 2010

Selected Element K courseware addresses Microsoft Certified Application Specialist skills for Microsoft Office. The following tables indicate where Word Expert 2010 skills are covered. For example, 3-A indicates the lesson and topic number applicable to that skill, and 3-1 indicates the lesson and activity number.

Objective Domain	Level	Topic	Activity
1.1 Configure Word options.			
1.1 1 Change default program options	1	1–B	1–2
1.1.2 Change spelling options	1	6–A	6–2
1.1.3 Change grammar checking options	1	6–A	
1.2 Apply protection to a document.			
1.2.1 Restrict editing	3	6–F	6–6
1.2.2 Apply controls or restrictions to document access	3	6–E, 6–F	6–5, 6–6
1.3 Apply a template to a document.			
1.3.1 Modify an existing template	2	8–A	8–1
1.3.2 Create a new template	2	8–B	8–2
1.3.3 Apply a template to an existing document	2	8–A	8–1
1.3.4 Manage templates by using the Organizer	2	10–A	
2.1 Apply advanced font and paragraph attributes.			
2.1.1 Use character attributes	1	3–A	3–1
2.1.2 Use character-specific styles	1	3–E	3–6
2.2 Create tables and charts.			
2.2.1 Insert tables by using Microsoft Excel data in tables	1	5–A	
2.2.2 Apply formulas or calculations on a table	2	2–C	2–3
2.2.3 Modify chart data	2	2–C	2–4
2.2.4 Save a chart as a template	2	2–D	
2.2.5 Modify chart layout	2	2–D	2–4
2.3 Construct reusable content in a document.			

Objective Domain	Level	Topic	Activity
2.3.1 Create customized building blocks	2	6–B	6–2
2.3.2 Save a selection as a quick part	2	6–B	6–2
2.3.3 Save quick parts after a document is saved	2	6–B	6–2
2.3.4 Insert text as a quick part	2	6–B	
2.3.5 Add content to a header or footer	2	6–D	
2.4 Link sections			
2.4.1 Link text boxes	2	7–D	7–4
2.4.2 Break links between text boxes	2	7–D	
2.4.3 Link different sections	2	7–B	
3.1 Review, compare, and combine documents.			
3.1.1 Apply tracking	3	2–C	2–3
3.1.2 Merge different versions of a document	3	3–C	3–3
3.1.3 Track changes in a combined document	3	2–E	2–6
3.1.4 Review comments in a combined document	3	2–F	2–7
3.2 Create a reference page.			
3.2.1 Add citations	3	4–F	4–6
3.2.2 Manage sources	3	4–F	4–7
3.2.3 Compile a bibliography	3	4–F	4–6
3.2.4 Apply cross references	3	4–E	4–5
3.3 Create a Table of Authorities in a document.			
3.3.1 Apply default formats	3	5–D	
3.3.2 Adjust alignment	3	5–D	
3.3.3 Apply a tab leader	3	5–D	
3.3.4 Modify style	3	5–D	5–6
3.3.5 Mark citations	3	5–D	5–5
3.3.6 Use passim (short form)	3	5–D	
3.4 Create an index in a document.			
3.4.1 Specify index type	3	5–B	
3.4.2 Specify columns	3	5–B	
3.4.3 Specify language	3	5–B	
3.4.4 Modify an index	3	5–B	
3.4.5 Mark index entries	3	5–B	5–2
4.1 Execute Mail Merge.			
4.1.1 Merge rules	2	9–A	
4.1.2 Send personalized email messages to multiple recipients	2	9–A	9–1
4.2 Create a Mail Merge by using other data sources.			

Objective Domain	Level	Topic	Activity
4.2.1 Use Microsoft Outlook tables as data source for a mail merge operation	2	9–A	
4.2.2 Use Access tables as data source for a mail merge operation	2	9–A	
4.2.3 Use Excel tables as data source for a mail merge operation	2	9–A	9–2
4.2.4 Use Word tables as data source for a mail merge operation	2	9–C	9–5
4.3 Create labels and forms.			
4.3.1 Prepare data	2	9–C	9–4
4.3.2 Create mailing labels	2	9–B	9–2
4.3.3 Create envelope forms	2	9–B	9–2
4.3.4 Create label forms	2	9–B	9–2
5.1 Apply and manipulate macros.			
5.1.1 Record a macro	2	10–B	10–2
5.1.2 Run a macro	2	10–A	10–1
5.1.3 Apply macro security	2	10–A	10–1
5.2 Apply and manipulate macro options.			
5.2.1 Run macros when a document is opened	2	10–A	
5.2.2 Run macros when a button is clicked	2	10–A	
5.2.3 Assign a macro to a command button	2	10–B	
5.2.4 Create a custom macro button on the Quick Access Toolbar	2	10–B	
5.3 Create forms.			
5.3.1 Use the Controls group	3	7–A	7–1
5.3.2 Add Help content to form fields	3	7–B	7–2
5.3.3 Link a form to a database	3	7–A	
5.3.4 Lock a form	3	7–B	7–2
5.4 Manipulate forms.			
5.4 1 Unlock a form	3	7–B	7–2
5.4 2 Add fields to a form	3	7–A	7–1
5.4 3 Remove fields from a form	3	7–A	

Lesson Labs

Lesson labs are provided as an additional learning resource for this course. The labs may or may not be performed as part of the classroom activities. Your instructor will consider setup issues, classroom timing issues, and instructional needs to determine which labs are appropriate for you to perform, and at what point during the class. If you do not perform the labs in class, your instructor can tell you if you can perform them independently as self-study, and if there are any special setup requirements.

Lesson 1 Lab 1

Creating a Word Document

Activity Time: 10 minutes

Scenario:

You work in the Human Resources department of a company. Your manager has given you his handwritten notes regarding a new HMO (Health Maintenance Organization) that will soon be available. You need to create an interoffice memo using the notes.

1. Launch the Microsoft Office Word application and open a new document.

2. Add the **Save As** and **Close All** commands to the Quick Access toolbar.

3. Create a tab and add the **Callout, Cancel,** and **Format Picture** commands to the tab.

4. Open a new blank document and set the view to Print Layout view.

5. In the new document, type *We will soon offer a new HMO plan with lower costs to all employees, but with the same coverage of the current plan. More details to come.*

6. Save the document as *My Memo* in the DOCX and DOC formats.

Lesson 2 Lab 1

Editing a Word Document

Activity Time: 10 minutes

Data Files:

Facility Request.docx, Building Security.docx, enus_084582_02_1_datafiles.zip

Scenario:

In your role, you need to edit procedure documents for the Human Resources department. You have the draft document to make the necessary changes. You need to insert some text, replace some existing text, and delete unwanted text to add more clarity to the documentation.

1. Open the Facility Request.docx file from the C:\084582Data\Editing Text in a Word Document\ folder.

2. Insert the text *(FRF),* in the first sentence, after the text "Facility Request Form."

3. Replace any remaining instances of "Facility Request Form" with "FRF."

4. Delete the paragraph that begins with "More than any other document."

5. Open the Building Security.docx file from the C:\084582Data\Editing a Word Document.

6. Copy the contact names and phone numbers from the end of the Building Security.docx file and close the file.

7. Paste the copied contact names and phone numbers in the Facility Request.docx file.

8. Save the document as *My Facility Request.docx* and close it.

Lesson 3 Lab 1

Formatting a Word Document

Activity Time: 10 minutes

Data Files:

C:\084582Data\Modifying the Appearance of Text in a Word Document\OGC Bookstore.docx, enus_084582_03_1_datfiles.zip

Scenario:

Your last assignment was successful. So, your manager at OGC Bookstore has entrusted you with a new task. She wants you to apply some formatting changes to one of her Word documents that she has saved as a draft to make it easier to read and visually appealing.

1. Open the OGC Bookstore.docx file from the C:\084582Data\Modifying the Appearance of Text in a Word Document folder.

2. Change the font style of the text to Arial.

3. Apply the **Heading 1** style to the heading "What Is OGC Bookstore" and center align the heading.

4. Apply the **Heading 2** style to the headings "Other Special Services," "How Are We Doing So Far?" and "Top Music Categories."

5. Change the paragraph spacing so that there is a 6-point space after each paragraph heading.

6. Format the paragraphs under the heading "Other Special Services" as a bulleted list.

7. Change the left indent of the tabbed text "Top Music Categories" to 1.5 inches, change the right indent to 4.5 inches, and center align the text.

8. Set the right tab stops in the tabbed text to stop at 3.25 inches and 4.25 inches.

9. Apply a box border to the "Top Music Categories" tabbed text.

10. Replace all the instances of text that have underline formatting applied with double-underlined, bold, and italic formatting.

11. Save the document as ***My OGC Bookstore*** in the DOCX format and close it.

Lesson 4 Lab 1

Inserting Graphic Elements

Activity Time: 10 minutes

Data Files:

C:\084582Data\Inserting Special Characters and Graphical Objects\Book.docx

Scenario:

You need to complete a one-page flyer promoting the upcoming "Get Published" seminar. You decide to include an appropriate image clip for the flyer and the corresponding copyright and trademark symbols.

1.   Open the Book.docx file from C:\084582Data\Inserting Special Characters and Graphical Objects folder.

2.   Insert a book-related image at the top of the document and resize it to keep the flyer to one page.

3.   In the first paragraph of the text, insert the corresponding symbols after the words "copyright" and "trademark."

4.   Save the document as ***My Book.docx*** and close it

Lesson 5 Lab 1

Adding Tables

Activity Time: 10 minutes

Data Files:

Music and Audio Books Sales.docx, enus_084582_05_1_datafiles.zip

Scenario:

Your coworker has asked you to create a table and format it according to the specifications of a reference document that she has handed to you. You also need to add a new table that includes various types of top-selling audio books.

1. Open the Music and Audio Books Sales.docx file from the C:\084582Data\Inserting Tables in a Word Document folder.

2. Convert the "Top Selling Music Categories" tabbed text into a table.

3. Format the table by using a table style and specifying other formatting options of your choice.

4. Create a table below the "Top Selling Audio Book Categories" heading to include the following details.

Category	Sales
Biography	1,589
Fiction	3,972
Hobby/Recreation	2,975
Youth	756

5. Apply a format to the new table so that its formatting matches the "Top Selling Music Categories" table.

6. Save the document as *My Music and Audio Books Sales* in the DOCX format and close it.

Lesson 6 Lab 1

Proofreading a Document

Activity Time: 10 minutes

Data Files:

Customer Letter.docx, enus_084582_06_1_datafiles.zip

Scenario:

You have completed a client letter and you want to proofread it before sending it out. You need to check for and correct typographical errors and make sure your grammar is correct. You also want to replace a word using the thesaurus, and check the word count to ensure it is within the limit.

1. Open the Customer Letter.docx file from the C:\084582Data\Proofing a Word Document folder.

2. Check the document for spelling and grammar errors and correct them as necessary.

3. Use the thesaurus to replace some instances of the word "business" with synonyms of your choice.

4. Verify that the letter has 200 words or fewer.

5. Save the document as *My Customer Letter* in the DOCX format and close it.

Lesson 7 Lab 1

Controlling the Appearance of a Page

Activity Time: 10 minutes

Data Files:

C:\084582Data\Controlling the Appearance of Pages in a Word Document\OGC Seminar.docx, enus_084582_07_1_datafiles.zip

Scenario:

The shop manager of your bookstore has provided you with some formatting suggestions for the seminar handouts that you have prepared for your bookstore. You need to implement those suggestions in the handout. Also, while previewing the document, you feel that the visual appeal of the document can be enhanced if you add a page color for the document.

1. Open the OGC Seminar.docx file from the C:\084582Data\Controlling the Appearance of the Pages in a Word Document folder.

2. Add a box border to the page.

3. Change the page color to a color of your choice.

4. Insert the date in the footer area.

5. Add a text watermark to the document.

6. Save the document as **My OGC Seminar** in the DOCX format and close it.

Lesson 8 Lab 1

Printing a Word Document

Activity Time: 10 minutes

Data Files:

C:\084582Data\Printing Word Documents\OGC Seminar.docx

Before You Begin:

Ensure that a printer is connected to your computer and that the necessary printer drivers are installed.

Scenario:

You have finished preparing a document. Before printing the document, you previewed it and found that there was no proper flow of the content layout. You need to specify the page layout settings so that the document appears as expected when it is printed.

---

1. Open the OGC Seminar.docx file from the C:\084582Data\Printing Word Documents folder.

---

2. Reduce the margins to fit the text on a single page.

---

3. Preview the document to verify the changes.

---

4. Print a copy of the document.

---

5. Save the document as *My OGC Seminar* in the DOCX format and close it.

Solutions

Activity 5-3

1. **Which group on the Table Tools Layout contextual tab includes the option to repeat the header rows?**

    ✓ a) The Data group

    b) The Rows & Columns group

    c) The Merge group

    d) The Table group

2. **True or False? The Row tab in the Table Properties dialog box has options to set the text wrapping of a table.**

    __ True

    ✓ False

Activity 5-5

1. **Which group on the Table Tools Design contextual tab has options to draw borders for a table?**

    a) The Table Style Options group

    ✓ b) Draw Borders group

    c) Table group

    d) Table Styles group

2. **Which tabs have options to insert and format a table?**

    ✓ a) The Insert tab

    b) The Home tab

    ✓ c) The Table Tools Design contextual tab

    d) The Table Tools Layout contextual tab

Glossary

AutoCorrect dialog box
A dialog box that provides options to control the behavior of the AutoCorrect feature in Word.

AutoCorrect
A feature that is used to fix common typographical errors.

AutoSave
A Word feature that saves your work automatically at a specified frequency so that you can recover your work later.

Backstage view
An interface that contains a series of tabs that group similar commands, and displays the compatibility, permissions, and version information of a Word document.

border
A decorative line or pattern applied around the objects to draw attention to them.

bulleted lists
The lists that are used to denote a group of equally significant items.

Check spelling and grammar as you type
A feature that displays a wavy red or wavy green underline below text that Word considers either a spelling or grammar error, respectively.

clip art
An illustration with a simple two-dimensional effect.

Clipboard task pane
A task pane that temporarily holds the objects that are copied or cut from another program.

Compatibility Checker feature
A feature that enables you to identify the compatibility of objects used in a .docx document when it is saved in an earlier version of Word.

delimiter
A delimiter is any character that is used to separate text while converting text into a table or table into text.

dialog box launchers
The small buttons that help you launch the relevant dialog boxes with advanced setting options.

dictionary
A list that is used to check the spelling of words in a document.

document template
A template that is used to create a specific type of document.

File tab
A Ribbon tab that contains options to perform common tasks such as opening, saving, closing, and printing a Word document.

font
A predefined typeface that can be used for displaying characters. Each font has a unique design and character spacing.

footer

The area in a page's bottom margin that can contain textual or graphical information. Ordinarily repeated throughout a document, a footer can be included only in some pages.

Format Painter

A formatting tool that allows you to duplicate the character or paragraph formatting in the selected text to a new text selection.

formatting marks

The document indicators that are nonprintable and are displayed in the text area.

global template

A template that stores settings that are available to all open documents.

header

The area in a page's top margin that can contain textual or graphical information. Ordinarily repeated throughout a document, a header can be included only in some pages.

Home tab

A Ribbon tab that contains the most commonly used commands that enable you to start working with a Word document.

illustrations

Graphic elements that provide visual representation of text.

indent

A technique to align the left and right edges of a paragraph without changing the margins for the entire document.

Insert tab

A Ribbon tab that enables quick access to different objects that can be inserted in a document.

line break

A formatting element that is used to end a line before it wraps to the next line without starting a new paragraph.

list

A data grouping method that displays the items in a group in a sequential manner.

Live Preview

A feature that enables users to preview the results before applying changes to document elements.

Mailings tab

A Ribbon tab that contains commands to create envelopes and labels.

margin

The blank area surrounding the text along the top, bottom, left, and right edges of a page.

Mini toolbar

A toolbar that contains commonly used commands for formatting text.

Navigation pane

A task pane that enables you to navigate to specific locations based on headings, subheadings, images and searched text.

numbered lists

The lists that are typically used to denote a ranking or a sequence to be followed.

page border

A formatting option that applies an outline to a document.

page break

An option that is used to split the content of a page at a specific location and move the remaining content to the next page automatically.

page color

A formatting option that applies a color shade to the background of a page.

Page Layout tab

A Ribbon tab that contains commands to customize the layout of the pages in a document.

page orientation

A page setup option that is used to control the layout of information on a page.

Paper size option

An option that is used to modify the width and height of a document to suit the paper used when printing.

paragraph alignment
An alignment technique that determines how a paragraph is positioned horizontally between the left and right margins.

picture
A graphic representation of a subject.

Quick Access toolbar
A toolbar that provides access to frequently used commands.

Quick Style set
A package of styles that can be applied to a document to change all the formatting in the document.

Readability Statistics dialog box
A dialog box that provides detailed information about a document, including counts and averages of words, characters, paragraphs, and sentences.

References tab
A Ribbon tab that contains options to add footnotes, captions, citations, bibliographies, index items, and many more.

Research task pane
A pane that allows you to look up information from a wide variety of online references.

Review tab
A Ribbon tab that provides various options to review and edit the contents in a document.

Ribbon
A panel that provides access to various commands.

rulers
The measuring tools that are used to align elements within a document.

Save As command
A command that is used to save an existing document with another file extension and in a new location.

Save command
A command that is used to save a newly created document or to save the changes made to an existing document.

ScreenTip
A short descriptive label that is displayed when you position the mouse pointer over Ribbon commands.

scroll bar
A bar used to navigate up, down, left, and right through a document.

shading
A proportion of color that can be imparted to the background of objects.

Smart tags
The tags applied to certain types of data such as names and dates on which specific actions can be performed.

special characters
Punctuation or typographical characters which are not available on a standard keyboard

status bar
A bar that displays options related to the functionality of a document.

symbols
The character marks that can be used to visually represent an idea or word.

tab stops
The document formatting options that allow you to align text to a specific horizontal location.

table style
A formatting option that contains sets of table-specific formatting options packaged together to apply design and formatting changes to a table all at once.

table
A container for text, data, or pictures that are stored in cells arranged in rows and columns.

tabs
See tab stops.

task pane
A small window within the Word environment that provides feature-specific options and commands.

thesaurus

A reference tool containing a collection of synonyms and antonyms.

title bar

A bar located at the top of the application window that displays the name of the document.

translation

A feature that allows you to translate the selected text into a different language.

View tab

A Ribbon tab that provides various options that enable you to switch between different document views.

watermark

A transparent reproduction of text or graphics that appears under the primary text that currently exists.

Word document

A document that is created by using the Microsoft Word application.

Word Help

A feature that provides you with a quick and easy way to find answers to Word-related queries.

Word Options dialog box

A dialog box that contains options to customize the Word environment.

Word style

A collection of appearance settings that can be applied to sections of a document as a group.

Word template

A predefined Word document that is used for the creation of other documents and templates.

Word Wrap

A data-entry feature that automatically wraps a long line of text around to the beginning of the next line.

Index

task Panes
  clip art, 126
thesaurus, 177
title bar, 4

V

views
  Draft, 21
  Full Screen Reading, 21
  Outline, 21
  Print Layout, 21
  Web Layout, 21
  Window, 22

W

watermarks, 193

Word document, 2
Word environment
  customizing, 13
Word Help, 7
Word Help pane, 8
Word Help toolbar, 8
Word Options dialog box, 13
Word styles, 95
Word templates, 20
  document, 20
  global, 20

select

SELECT **YOUR PATH TO LEARNING**

For over 30 years, Logical Operations has provided the highest-quality training programs designed for your specific needs. From the beginning, we've been committed to offering the most up-to-date and relevant education and training curriculum that are designed for your selected professional learning path.

Training should empower you to develop to the best of your abilities, to learn the critical skills needed to become highly effective at your job, advance your career, and experience greater professional fulfillment. SELECT enables you to select your own professional learning path through a wide variety of established training curriculums.

No two individuals learn the same way and no two professional training paths are the same. Discover your unique path to success through SELECT.

Book

eBook

Assessment

3535 Winton Place
Rochester, NY 14623

www.logicaloperations.com

084582 S3 rev 1.0
ISBN-13 978-1-4246-1644-2
ISBN-10 1-4246-1644-1

90000

9 781424 616442

This Journal Belongs to:

JOURNAL FOR THE HEART
published by Multnomah Publishers, Inc.

© 2000 by Alice Gray
International Standard Book Number: 1-57673-684-9

Cover photograph by Superstock
Design by Stephen Gardner

Multnomah is a trademark of Multnomah Publishers, Inc.,
and is registered in the U.S. Patent and Trademark Office.
The colophon is a trademark of Multnomah Publishers, Inc.

Quote by Nancy Spiegelberg. Used by permission of the author. www.godthoughts.com.

Quote by Philip Yancey. Used by permission of the author
and Multnomah Publishers, Inc., Sisters, OR. 97759

"Faith Is…" by Pamela Reeve. Excerpted from *Faith Is…* by Pamela Reeve © 1994 Multnomah
Publishers, Inc., Sisters, OR 97759. Used by permission of the publisher.

Quotes by C.R. Gibson Company excerpted from *Words I Have Lived By* by Norman Vincent Peale
© 1990. Used by permission of C.R. Gibson Company, 39 Knight Street, Norwalk, CT 06856

Quotes by Heartland Samplers excerpted from *Bless Your Heart series 1* flip calendar. © 1987. Used
by permission of Heartland Samplers, Inc., 3255 Springs St. N.E., Minneapolis, MN 55413

Printed in China

For information:
MULTNOMAH PUBLISHERS, INC.
POST OFFICE BOX 1720
SISTERS, OREGON 97759

00 01 02 03 04 05 06 — 10 9 8 7 6 5 4 3 2 1

Journal for the Heart

BASED ON ALICE GRAY'S BESTSELLING SERIES
STORIES FOR THE HEART

Multnomah®Publishers *Sisters, Oregon*

A smile of encouragement at the right moment
may act like sunlight on a closed-up flower;
it may be the turning point for a struggling life.

Kind words are the music of the world.

They have power that seems to be beyond natural causes,

as if they were some angel's song that had lost its way and come on earth.

—FREDERICK WILLIAM FABER

*Lighthouses don't ring bells and fire guns to
call attention to their light...they just shine!*

You will find as you look back upon your life, that the moments when you have really lived are the moments when you have done things in the spirit of love.

—HENRY DRUMMOND

*In times of affliction we commonly meet with
the sweetest experiences of the love of God.*

—JOHN BUNYAN

And now these three remain: faith, hope and love.
But the greatest of these is love.

—PAUL THE APOSTLE

God pardons like a mother, who kisses the offense into everlasting forgiveness.

—HENRY WARD BEECHER

I long to put the experience of fifty years into your young lives, to give you at once the key of that treasure chamber every gem of which has cost me tears and struggles and prayer; but you must work for these inward treasures yourselves.

—HARRIET BEECHER STOWE

Love one another deeply from the heart.

1 PETER 1:22

Trust people as if they were what they ought to be
and you help them become what they are capable of being.

—GOETHE

The human soul is a silent harp in God's choir, whose strings need only to be
swept by the divine breath to chime in with the harmonies of creation.

—HENRY DAVID THOREAU

The art of being happy lies in the power of extracting happiness from common things.

—HENRY WARD BEECHER

Have courage for the great sorrows of life and patience for the small ones;
and when you have laboriously accomplished your daily task, go to sleep in peace.
God is awake.

—VICTOR HUGO

Some of God's attributes are too wonderful to understand.
But even if they remain darkness to the intellect,
let them be sunshine for your soul.

The greatest thing in the world is not so much where we stand as in what direction we're moving.

—OLIVER WENDELL HOLMES

O God of Second Chances and New Beginnings,
Here I am again.

—NANCY SPIEGELBERG

He drew a circle that shut me out—Heretic, rebel, a thing to flout.
But Love and I had the wit to win; We drew a circle that took him in!

—EDWIN MARKHAM

In dreams and love there are no impossibilities.

—JANOS ARANY

Above all else, guard your heart, for it is the wellspring of life.

—PROVERBS 4:23

We are shaped and fashioned by what we love.

—GOETHE

I believe in the sun even when it is not shining.

I believe in love even when I feel it not.

I believe in God even when He is silent.

—WRITTEN ON A WALL IN A CONCENTRATION CAMP

Where your pleasure is, there is your treasure.
Where your treasure is, there is your heart.
Where your heart is, there is your happiness.

—AUGUSTINE

The human heart yearns for the beautiful in all ranks of life.

—HARRIET BEECHER STOWE

How far you go in life depends on your being tender with the young, compassionate with the aged, sympathetic with the striving, and tolerant of the weak and the strong—because someday you will have been all of these.

—GEORGE WASHINGTON CARVER

Blessed is the man who has the gift of making friends; for it is one of God's best gifts. It involves many things, but above all the power of going out of one's own self and seeing and appreciating whatever is noble and loving in another man.

—THOMAS HUGHES

When one door closes, another opens.
But we often look so regretfully upon the closed door
That we don't see the one that has opened for us.

—ALEXANDER GRAHAM BELL

I am full-fed and yet I hunger. What means this deeper hunger in my heart?

—ALFRED NOYES, C.R. GIBSON COMPANY

Few delights can equal the mere presence of one whom we trust utterly.

—GEORGE MACDONALD

When I pray, coincidences happen.
When I stop praying, coincidences stop.

—WILLIAM TEMPLE, ARCHBISHOP OF CANTERBURY

*If all our misfortunes were laid in one common heap,
most people would be contented to take their own and depart.*

For he will command his angels concerning you,
to guard you in all your ways.

PSALM 91:11

Because God has made us for Himself,
our hearts are restless until they rest in Him.

—SAINT AUGUSTINE

What sunshine is to flowers, smiles are to humanity.
They are but trifles to be sure, but scattered along life's pathway,
the good they do is inconceivable.

—JOSEPH ADDISON

Let my heart be broken with the things that break the heart of God.

—ROBERT W. PIERCE

Love comforteth like sunshine after rain.

—WILLIAM SHAKESPEARE

Every morning lean your arms awhile upon the window sill of heaven
And gaze upon the Lord.
Then, with the vision in your heart
Turn strong to meet your day.

In times like these, it helps to recall that there have always been times like these.

—PAUL HARVEY, C.R. GIBSON COMPANY

*Our friends see the best in us, and by
that very fact call forth the best from us.*

—HUGH BLACK

When we feel as if God is nowhere, He is watching over us with an eternal consciousness, above and beyond our every hope and fear.

—GEORGE MACDONALD

After two weeks of reading the entire Bible,
I came away with the strong sense that God does not
care so much about being analyzed. Mainly, he wants to be loved.

—PHILIP YANCEY

If I can stop one heart from breaking, I shall not live in vain.
If I can ease one life the aching, or cool one pain,
Or help one fainting robin into his nest again, I shall not live in vain.

—EMILY ELIZABETH DICKINSON

Come to me, all you who are weary and burdened, and I will give you rest.

—MATTHEW 11:28

We are like angels with just one wing.
We fly only by embracing each other.

Faith is...

Remembering I am God's priceless treasure when I feel utterly worthless.

—PAMELA REEVE, FROM "FAITH IS"

If a man does not keep pace with his companions,

perhaps it is because he hears a different drummer.

Let him step to the music which he hears, however measured or far away.

—HENRY DAVID THOREAU

Henceforth there will be such a oneness between us—
That when one weeps the other will taste salt.

God gave us memories so
that we might have roses in December.

It is when we forget ourselves
that we do things that will be remembered.

Faith is the bird that feels
the light and sings
while the dawn is yet dark.

—TAGORE

A friend will strengthen you with her prayers,
bless you with her love, and encourage you with her heart.

Fear not tomorrow for God is already there.

If you have much, give of your wealth;
If you have little, give of your heart.

Happiness resides not in possessions and not in gold;
The feeling of happiness dwells in the soul.

—DEMOCRITUS

A faithful friend is a sturdy shelter.
He that has found one
Has found a treasure.

ECCLESIASTES 6:14

Hope is brightest
When it dawns from fears.

—SIR WALTER SCOTT

I breathed a song into the air, It fell to earth I know not where...
And the song from beginning to end, I found again in the heart of a friend.

—HENRY WADSWORTH LONGFELLOW

*If instead of a gem, or even a flower, we should cast the gift of
a loving thought into the heart of a friend—that would be giving as the angels give.*

—GEORGE MACDONALD

Touched by a loving heart, Wakened by kindness,
Chords that were broken, Will vibrate once more.

—FANNY CROSBY

The heart is its own memory, like the mind, and in it are enshrined precious keepsakes, into which is wrought the giver's loving touch.

—HENRY WADSWORTH LONGFELLOW

It takes two to speak truth—one to speak, and another to listen.

—HENRY DAVID THOREAU

"Oh, how delightful it would be to live in a house where everybody understood, and loved, and thought about everybody else!" She did not know that she was wishing for nothing more and something a little less than the kingdom of heaven.

—GEORGE MACDONALD

If we fill our hours with regrets of yesterday and worries of tomorrow,
we have no today in which to be thankful.

If I had a single flower for every time I think about you,
I could walk forever in my garden.

—CLAUDIA GRANDI

If I were to be described in one word, what would it be?

Fragrance always clings to the hand that gives you roses.

—CHINESE PROVERB

Happiness comes of the capacity to feel deeply,
to enjoy simply, to think freely, to risk life and to be needed.

—STORM JAMISON

It is right to be contented with what we have, never with what we are.

—MACKINTOSH

Take time to laugh. It is the music of the soul.

—ANONYMOUS

Friendship that flows from the heart cannot be frozen by adversity,
as the water that flows from the spring cannot congeal in winter.

—JAMES FENIMORE COOPER

The smallest seed of faith is better than the largest fruit of happiness.

—HENRY DAVID THOREAU

Laughter is the best medicine for a long and happy life. He who laughs—lasts.

—WILFRED PETERSON

Life is short and we never have enough time for gladdening the hearts of those who travel the way with us. Oh, be swift to love. Make haste to be kind.

—HENRI FREDERIC AMIEL

Delight yourself in the Lord and he will give you the desires of your heart.

—PSALM 37:4

Forgiveness is the fragrance the violet sheds on the heel that has crushed it.

—MARK TWAIN

Lord of my heart's elation, Spirit of things unseen,
Be thou my aspiration, Consuming and serene!

—HENRY WADSWORTH LONGFELLOW

One can never consent to creep when one feels an impulse to soar.

—HELEN KELLER, C. R. GIBSON COMPANY

He who cannot forgive breaks the bridge over which he himself must pass.

—GEORGE HERBERT

The real voyage of discovery consists not in seeking new landscapes but in having new eyes.

—MARCEL PROUST